Bridging the Opportunity Gap

Leadership, Social Difference,
Career and Education

Dr. Danielle Hyles-Rainford

iUniverse, Inc.
Bloomington

To my daughter, Vivien Nicole Rainford

Bridging the Opportunity Gap
Leadership, Social Difference, Career and Education

iUniverse books may be ordered through booksellers or by contacting:

iUniverse
1663 Liberty Drive
Bloomington, IN 47403
www.iuniverse.com
1-800-Authors (1-800-288-4677)

Because of the dynamic nature of the Internet, any Web addresses or links contained in this book may have changed since publication and may no longer be valid. The views expressed in this work are solely those of the author and do not necessarily reflect the views of the publisher, and the publisher hereby disclaims any responsibility for them.

Any people depicted in stock imagery provided by Thinkstock are models, and such images are being used for illustrative purposes only.

Certain stock imagery © Thinkstock.

ISBN: 978-1-4502-8827-9 (sc)
ISBN: 978-1-4502-8828-6 (dj)
ISBN: 978-1-4502-8829-3 (e)

Library of Congress Control Number: 2011900423

Printed in the United States of America

iUniverse rev. date: 1/17/2012

CONTENTS

ACKNOWLEDGEMENTS

During the course of writing this book, my husband, Marc Rainford and I got married and had our precious baby girl, Vivien. Without his loving support, this book would not have been possible. I would like to take this opportunity to acknowledge key individuals who have nurtured, inspired and intellectually challenged me to continue in my work. Dr. Peter Sawchuk, Dr. Njoki Wane, Dr. George Dei, Dr. Sue Grant Lewis, Dr. Clarence Lee, Ambassador Horace G. Dawson, Dr. Gail Dale-Young, Zillous Byer, Violet Marin, and Dianne Hyles, my mother, who by example have taught me that the level of struggle one experiences can equate the level of positive contribution one makes to the world. To Dr. Chris Spence, whose passionate life models success in career navigation of school systems for the sole purpose of infusing and producing equitable outcomes for all students. He is now the Director of Education for the Toronto District School Board (TDSB). I am truly thankful to Karen Falconer, Superintendent of Education in the TDSB, who has been instrumental in my growth as a professional. Karen has supported countless professionals in their career journey, she has made it her personal mission to cultivate, mentor and empower aspiring leaders including all marginalized groups to succeed. I gratefully acknowledge the contributions of Jack Nigro, Pardeep Nagra, Carol Soper, Beverly MacRae, Jana Vinsky, and my father-in-law, Anthony Rainford, who spent many hours offering valuable suggestions that have improved this work.

A special mention to all of the marginalized professionals including visible minorities and women educators whom I have met over the years who candidly shared their trials and tribulations towards school leadership promotion in Canada and in other international contexts, which instinctively motivated me to do this type of research. My sincere gratitude to the fifteen vice principals and principals in Ontario, Canada and the fifteen head masters and mistresses of elementary schools in Koforidua, Ghana who gave of their time, experience and sentiments around school promotion and their professional endeavours. The overall goal is to empower visible minorities, women and others who confront barriers to use agency and navigational tools to allow them to succeed in their promotion to elementary school principal. By using their credentials or human capital, political astuteness, organizational networks or social capital, and know-how with the checks-and-balances in the education system, their cultural capital, visible minorities and women have agency, resilience and personal power to confront barriers that are entrenched in the education system. Observed through the study both Ghanaian and Ontarian school boards are currently and actively working on bridging the opportunity gap in school leadership; some by using demographic data to analyze representation in all levels and for all employees in a school board.

The truth of the matter is that this generation of children and the next generation need to see visible minorities and women in school leadership positions so, they can aspire to become a school principal. The lack of representation speaks volumes to a child's subconscious in what they perceive as a realistic dream. If there are no role models around, it would be difficult for a visible minority child or girl to conceive of this dream. This is why this study is so important, today.

FOREWORD

Bridging the Opportunity Gap is an important study that analyses the career paths of many who struggled to overcome systemic barriers to promotion. Conversations addressing the career mobility of "minorities" are challenging because it is often difficult to isolate many of the factors which prevent promotion, this study dares to be different as Dr. Danielle Hyles-Rainford tackles three notions of career mobility: the career ladder (the vertical climb), the spiral (balancing pace and skill set) and the web (the importance of people). She clearly compares the Canadian and Ghanaian educators who have and who have not made inroads maneuvering these complexities and then she effectively delineates the factors that contribute to the success of those who persevere.

Seeking promotion will always be a gamble; therefore those not representing the dominant power group will need tools to successfully navigate systems that are too often reluctant to probe the tough questions of race, gender, class and ethnicity and their correlation to the characteristics of the success group. The author has proposed a Conscious Career Elevation Model that seeks to address these tough issues in career advancement in a methodical and well-prescribed manner. This model provides a roadmap to tackle social barriers and marginalization insomuch as they impact on career progression in an educational organization. Through careful analyses of attributes of human, social and cultural capital in both Canada and Ghana, the author has developed a strategy that will maximize opportunities for promotion and will serve as an excellent tool for mentoring.

There is no doubt that that the dominant group feels strongly that the path to career mobility is through high competence, significant knowledge and some luck. Notable studies in this area, as well as our empirical evidence, suggest that much more than this is required for marginalized groups to be as successful as their dominant group counterparts. It is gratifying to have Dr. Hyles-Rainford point us in a forward direction with the use of navigational tools that are easy to understand and even easier to use.

Dr. Chris Spence Director of Education Toronto District School Board

Karen Falconer Superintendent of Education Toronto District School Board

PREFACE

This study investigates and analyzes the experiences of elementary school principals and the processes they underwent in their promotion from educator to principal: that is, it interrogates the notion of career mobility in school systems. The purpose of conducting this study was to explore the social barriers that impede the career mobility of aspiring elementary educators, with a specific focus on race and gender. Previous research in the field of mobility and leadership in education has rarely brought together issues of race, gender and identity politics with the notions of human, social and cultural capital accumulation. Specifically, studies to date have not identified the impact of race, gender and other social identity intersectionalities in terms of school promotion, and determine what attributes are associated with career success. As a response to those gaps I argue for a model of multiple forms of capital (human, social and cultural) that mediate and mutually constitute one another to produce the simultaneously racialized, gendered, classed and other marginalized experiences and outcomes of educational career mobility.

Using a cross-cultural comparative and narrative methodological approach supported by survey-styled data, in-depth interviews and observations within qualitative research traditions, and using a social, human and cultural capital theoretical framework, the study investigates 15 Ghanaian elementary school principals and 15 Canadian elementary school principals. The principals consulted had varied entry points and access to promotional opportunities. Through this triangular approach of individual interviews, survey-styled data and observations, all supplemented by relevant research, the study provides professional and personal insights to help marginalized groups such as visible minorities and women educator candidates, across two distinct cultural/national settings to enhance their understanding of the system as well as to gain access to higher level positions of school leadership. The Canadian and Ghanaian study participants were of diverse racial/ethnic backgrounds, age range, gender, school boards and denominations, and class. Some key findings were: horizontal mobility is valued in Canada and not in Ghana; Canadian and Ghanaian respondents show reluctance to acknowledge under-representation of visible minority groups/ethnicities in school leadership positions; and female participants did report delays in career due to family/childrearing. The Conscious Career Elevation model is an agency tool created.

INTRODUCTION

We are all situated in various positions and dispositions when trying to place ourselves in a uniquely structured system of education. Our positions and dispositions encompass political or physical identities such as race, ethnic background, gender, age, socio-economic status, religion, (dis) ability, and sexuality. However, this information should not be the only defining dimension to the position or upward mobility status when trying to gain access to promotion within school leadership. Your pace or personal journey to success and failure for the attainment of career mobility has personal traits of notable recognition that many successful educators have applied and triumphed in their dreams, goals and ambitions to becoming a school principal. This work will argue that there are trends in personal traits and professional attributes that are common to all regardless of their position and disposition within the institution of education. Moreover, it will attempt to recognize the social difference barriers including race and gender within a human, social and cultural capital framework to see how marginalized groups such as visible minority educators and women can gain access to positions of school leadership. Historical and present accounts and realities attest to the difficulties minoritized professionals faced when attempting to be promoted to school leadership.

In addition, this body of work tries to have a clear understanding of the complexity of race and gender issues within two cross-cultural contexts such as Ghana and Canada. The first goal is to provide personal and professional agency to those who have experienced resistance, discrimination, alienation or sabotage in their journey to promotion. However, this experience may not be in the consciousness or awareness of those in positions of power. The various levels of consciousness could be understood as an "information gap". Ann Perron (2010), the second female Director of Education at the Toronto Catholic District School Board, discusses the information gap that we all must fill to have proper governance to instill public confidence for all education stakeholders. Aligned with the "information gap", the second goal of the study is also to give agency to those who are just embarking on their promotional process who are currently experiencing the barriers embedded within the education system.

This work is crucial to eliminate barriers in order for the next generation of visible minority, female and all other minoritized groups of students' to have full access and equity in their school leadership promotional endeavours. Just as the student achievement gap serves this disparity, the first African-Canadian Director of Education at the Toronto District School Board, Dr. Chris Spence (2009) states "this *opportunity gap* exists when specific groups of students do not achieve in school at the same level. Achievement gaps may correlate with race, ethnicity, family income level, language background, ability/disability status, and gender. However, principals must remember that correlation is not causation." If we do not make the connection between the current student *achievement gap* which will result in widening their future "opportunity gap", these systemic, social difference barriers and attitudes of those in power will continue to repeat itself in the next generation. There needs to be representation at all levels of the education system in order for our students to not experience the limitations, barriers or ceilings that their adult role models experienced. Our students can only dream of what they can conceive, believe and achieve through the examples of the educators around them or in their direct experience. The time is now to address these issues and find supports for our pupils and practitioners to circumvent barriers and rise to greater positions of leadership and community mobilization for student achievement. The practical suggestion of this research revolves around the hope of providing navigational tools to empower marginalized professionals, simultaneously providing positive models or our students to imprint higher dreams and aspirations that should be evident and infused in their everyday environment.

Race To The Top Case Study

Race to the Top is a double entendre for the race to make it, otherwise known as the *fast track*. The race reference is the *race card*, your physical appearance, assignment of race, identity and ethnic origin. The inner drive to achieve, the motivation to succeed and its pace is regulated by one's inner compass and individualism versus social constructed nature of difference, barriers and supports. The career journey has both failure and triumph, all a learning process for promotional attainment. The *fast track* is commonly referred to as the career treadmill. Once you are on it; it is difficult to *get off*. Ironically, it is also simultaneously difficult to maintain the pace, exertion of ability and determination to achieve human, social and cultural capital accumulation. This work will provide a more focused comparison between Ghanaian and Canadian respondents in terms of: career mobility, school leadership, politics within the organization, social difference including factors of race and gender as well as the interactions between human, social and cultural capital. By way of introducing these interactions and the other themes covered, I want to begin with a brief vignette entitled *Race to the Top*: a composite of the experiences of educators from across the data set condensed into one story. Its purpose is to help sensitize the reader to the complexity and simultaneity of the dynamics explored.

Enza, a Ghanaian immigrant graduated from a Canadian teacher's college with an elementary language education focus, she had a number of interviews for positions on the elementary panel but never got an offer. She recalled an occasion where one of the interviewers had commented as the interview was about to begin, 'your resume is really strong to have gotten this far; usually we don't get many non-native speakers at this stage in the game'. Enza remembered how difficult it was for her to overlook the remark and keep her indignation in check—after all she needed the job. She recalled how she actually thought about ways she would address such attitude once she was on the inside. She never did hear back from that school, but finally did manage to get a teaching position. During her first week on the job, she quickly came to know the circumstances around her hiring. Apparently the decision had come down to two candidates: Enza and Scott, an older teacher who had worked part-time at the school over the past year helping out wherever needed. Enza came to know from staff room whisperings and informal conversations with colleagues that some of the teachers at the school felt that Scott should have been offered the position. These teachers felt that if it had not been for calls for 'diversity amongst the staff', Scott would have been hired.

As the first school year unfolded, Enza quietly established herself as a student favourite. Many of the school's immigrant and visible minority students identified positively with Enza and felt she understood their own cultural and linguistic challenges. Her skills and popularity did not always sit well with some staff members who still saw Enza as undeserving of her position. Enza could sense their reservations as articulated in staff committee meetings or on the staff discussion list. Remarks like, "the right person doesn't always get the job", or "we've got to have token representation, don't we?" said in the course of conversations about other people and situations always left questions in Enza's mind about their intended purposes. Were those veiled comments addressed at her?

....

The sudden sound of the intercom rattled Enza out of her momentary journey down memory lane and back to the immediacy of the situation at hand. Naomi was on the intercom informing Enza that everyone for her 2:30 meeting had arrived and assembled in the conference room. After twelve years as a teacher and several failed attempts at becoming a vice-principal, Enza had finally got her break when the board proposed a new school in the heart of its immigrant population. Now, as principal she was finally able to implement her vision to create a pluralistic school culture, a diverse staff, and a commitment to transparent administrative practices. The staff at this new school had become increasingly diverse. However, it had become painfully obvious that there was divisiveness amongst staff members and it often centered on notions of equity. Today's staff meeting in the school library was an outcome of issues that had accelerated into a rift between members of her teaching staff regarding the newly integrated Action for Diversity and Inclusion school board policy and how it would apply to the selection of the new permanent Vice Principal. The search committee was comprised of Mr. Swartz, a regional superintendent, Ms. Chan, a long-serving principal, and Enza.

After interviewing a large pool of candidates for the position, the search committee had narrowed the candidacy to two professionals. The search committee met for their final time to make their decision. Enza reviewed a synopsis of both candidates. The first candidate Mrs. Yaa was a Canadian born Ghanaian whose family had migrated from Ghana. She has several years of teaching experience in different grade levels and in schools with diverse student populations. However, she had only recently completed the principal course and received her certification. The second candidate Mr. Smith is a fourth generation Canadian with Irish heritage. He has similar teaching experience including special education and has been a Vice Principal for three years in a suburban area with a fairly homogenous student body.

Enza's own reflections on the matter leading up to the meeting had left her feeling conflicted. She thought about how the committee's decision would be perceived by the different groups on her staff. She also knew that others, outside her school, were keenly observing the process and the decision. She was acutely sensitive to how others would react to her personal position on the matter—her work over the years on diversity within the profession had resulted in creating supporters and detractors alike. Most of them would agree, however, that Enza was a highly principled individual. One minority teacher in the school, who she particularly respected, had made it a point of shaking Enza's hand earlier in the day, saying "I am glad we have someone like you who is supporting us minorities in gaining higher positions." Naomi, her trusted school secretary, approached Enza and said "I have always admired how you are fair and can discern the wheat from the shaff? I know you will choose the best qualified professional for the job." The pressure was mounting.

At the meeting, the regional superintendent Mr. Swartz made a case for Mrs. Yaa and pointed out that her diversity expertise would complement the needs of the students in this school and thus, was a better fit; she would get his vote. Then, Ms. Chan quickly spoke out for Mr. Smith and suggested that he was clearly better qualified for this position and would get her vote. As the tension rose in the room, Ms. Chan remarked, "You want to choose the best qualified candidate, don't you. I know you are not the kind of Principal that would let other factors get in the way." Mr. Swartz quickly went to Enza's defense "Ms. Chan, as a visible minority won't it benefit the school to have multiple visible minorities in leadership? This is almost unheard of in this school board but the search committee can make this happen." Mr. Swartz and Ms. Chan were clearly divided on the issue; they had indicated their preferences. The matter now rested with Enza, as she would have to cast the deciding vote. Enza thanked both of the committee members for their thoughtful arguments. There was

an uncomfortable silence in the room before Enza gave her answer.
(Syed, Zafar, Danielle Hyles, and Andrea Jenkins, 2006)

What would you do if you were Enza?

To unpack the interactions of this vignette, there are many social variables that Enza had to challenge. Some of these interactions were:

(1) How one's own history and experience of discrimination can inform and impact decision-making and enhance one's deconstruction of power and privilege within the political structure of a school board, equity policies and procedures, issues around meritocracy, influential support from key stakeholders for visible minorities and internalized racism.

(2) This vignette sets a context to magnify the voices of aspiring teacher leaders who are experiencing multiple forms of marginalization. These are the voices of the racialized bodies, women or people who come from low-socioeconomic backgrounds, immigrant populations and the young and capable who are silenced in their professions and who desperately need to be heard.

(3) There are core contradictions and silent assumptions that speak to the social difference of race, gender and how cultural capital manifests. The core contradictions are that privileged groups support their own and that visible minorities support one another; this is true to some extent.

(4) In the vignette, however, we see that Mr. Swartz supporting Mrs. Yaa (a superintendent in a privileged group supporting a visible minority) and Mrs. Chan (an established visible minority principal who does not support a woman or another visible minority). For all parties involved in this decision-making process, the predominant factors within the committees own personal histories to attain their position may have influenced their thought process such as experiencing situations of praise and merit or racial and/or gender discrimination.

(5) Regardless, it is critical to understand that there is a myriad of standpoints that professionals operate from and reason for their decisions.

(6) In addition, it is essential to understand that the vignette exposes individual agency and the importance of having key allies that understand the barriers that exist within the system, school and internal or external cultural networks. Agency has many shapes and forms. One can find like-minded individuals in powerful positions and at all levels of a school board that one may approach to join in the cause of eliminating anti-discriminatory practices.

(7) Lastly, in the selection process we can ask about the role of objectivity and equitably specified criteria? There are standardized qualifications, i.e., human capital; however, there is also the school board and the administrator's priorities and agendas whose aim is to make this a seamless transition. Therefore, with all of the competing agendas the process of selection is rarely an ideal democratic process.

Keeping in mind the interactions of this vignette, this chapter serves to disclose the dilemmas and dichotomies that social difference, leadership and career mobility aspirations for elementary school practitioners in Ghana and Canada experience.

Chapter 1

Educators Swimming Upstream

*Leaders hear and incorporate the agenda – but often in
ways that extend beyond the particulars-find and seize upon
common visions yet extend the horizons of possibility.*

(Carol Ann Tomlinson & Susan Demirsky Allen, 2000)

This chapter provides an entry point for the critical examination of social difference and inequity that influence career mobility aspirations for elementary school practitioners. To understand the blueprint of the study, it is important to understand the architect: the researcher and her personal location. The architect designs the plans of the study. Historically, many marginalized professionals including visible minorities and women have been denied access to positions of responsibility in school leadership. Today, there remain threads of barriers to accessing these positions of added responsibility such as elementary school principal. There are serious implications for the next generation. The current marginalized students including visible minority and girls have a stake in this complex problem involving lack of access, equity and representation within educational promotion.

This study explores the factors that implicate social difference and career mobility access for elementary school practitioners, asking if there are built-in mechanisms in the elementary education system working to keep marginalized professionals including visible minorities and women off the promotional ladder? If so, this suggests a repeating cycle sustaining and mutually reinforcing set of hegemonic ideologies in school leadership; and simultaneously will reveal agency attributes and navigational tools. While paying particular attention to the architect's identity politics in an increasingly neo-liberal landscape, the researcher's plan encompasses her politics, reviews theoretical and empirical research. This connects the research back to the larger plan which shapes the direction of the innovation created; the new blueprint expounding on a previous notion and making contributions to the field.

This chapter will frame the relevance of the study for education professionals and will help us to grapple with its necessity at this time when marginalized individuals are becoming increasingly educated and will continue to knock on the school boards' doors for school leadership promotions. With this context in mind, the material in this chapter is informed by the following objectives:

1. How do the three central research questions impact aspiring educators and current students, the next generation of educators?
2. What are the limitations and implications of the study for marginalized professionals with regard to career mobility?

In order to address these questions, this chapter is organized as follows:
I.   Multi-Positioned Location
II.   Multi-Positionality and the Study
III. Sketching the Study
IV.   Educators Flowing Through History: Ripples, Waves and Rapid Waters
V.   Structuring the Flow of the Study
VI.   Hearing the Voices of Principals Through Data
VII. Research Challenges and Possibilities

Multi-Positioned Location

Upon reflecting on an analogy based on a forest metaphor, when you look at a forest in the distance, it is like looking at your community of trees. Yet, as you walk closer you see that all of the individual trees are placed at different locations in your community, resulting in the uniqueness of *positionality*. Keeping in mind, *intersectionalities* such as race, gender, class and age, we can see an individual tree as growing complicated with thorns and flower buds, with different levels of aliveness that shift depending on context. Understanding that *positionality* is shifting, contextual and fluid, the effects of social class, human capital accumulation, striving goals of educational attainment, age and gender can be both a mixture of flower buds and thorns. Positionality morphs again, at another level such as marital status, being foreign or Canadian born, immigration status, place of origin, ethnicity and race. The complex and fluid nature of identity and its politics, drawing on this metaphor of the forest, is why I feel one's unique location needs to be heard. It is important to take the time and reflect on your own positionality, grounded in your *identity politics* to see how you can be read in your current organization. This is the piece of the inequity puzzle we can resonate with. What are your multi-positionalities in your personal and professional identity? What tension does your multi-positioned location evoke in your career aspirations and your daily interactions?

> *My intended contribution in terms of research insights, content, concepts and principles reflect all marginality in the school system to inform and help navigate a successful path to school leadership.*

"All of *us* are multi-positioned, implicated in unequally empowered ways of understanding and doing; people share positioning in common and yet are not simply defined by sets of binaries; black/white, working class/middle class, female/male" (Arber, 2000). We all inhabit many unequally empowered positions. As a multi-positioned elementary educator and now administrator, I have been preoccupied with this perplexing phenomenon of seeing some marginalized professionals including visible minorities and women being denied opportunities to advance in their chosen career. They have the relevant experience, credentials, qualifications and academic achievements, as well as political and social astuteness; however, they can and still are denied access to higher level positions.

I would like to research the question: what barriers in the education system halt marginalized educators from gaining access to school leadership promotion and what empowerment tools can assist in circumventing these barriers? However, I would like to also develop applicable tools for marginalized professionals. In this study I ask questions that explore the attributes aspiring educators need, the criteria that inform career decisions, and how these relate to the systemic and highly interactive sets of barriers that prevent career mobility for some professionals in elementary education. Our challenge is to understand our own entry-point as a professional in the education system, with the societal advantages and disadvantages, and to engage elementary school administrators in a discourse that benefits all who have a stake.

In my experience as an international educator, the presence of social barriers appeared to be reinforced in the systems evidenced in the study. I actively began to seek out people and have informal conversations to ask them about what they experienced, and ask how the presence of social barriers was affecting and not affecting their careers. I received a range of responses about how women were mistreated, or being discounted for their age or rejected for their class and/or the village they live in, or being ostracized because of their race in many nations, foreign or otherwise such as England, South Africa, Brazil, United States, India, Japan, etc. This compelled me to consider another layer in my research -- a cross-cultural one. By experiencing other people's realities and oppressions in other places and comparing them to those in Canada, I decided to choose Koforidua, Ghana and Ontario, Canada to compare. I chose Ghana because of its unique history, being the first African nation south of the Sahara to gain independence from colonial rule. It was also the first post-colonial African country to begin the re-appropriation and reconstruction of its education system. In addition, Ghana is the country from where the descendents of my own ancestors from Trinidad and Tobago where forcefully relocated via the Middle Passage: a fact I learned visiting the Elmina Castle, the Slave Trade Dungeon in Ghana. This particular cross-cultural comparison is reflective of the historical roots of my own identity, and it offers an ideal location to make cross-cultural comparisons. Specifically, it offers a chance to see if visible minorities and women from various cultural and socio-economic backgrounds experienced some of the same educational career mobility barriers, and how that compares to visible minorities and women educators in Ontario. In Ghana, I explored how, despite independence, elements of colonial practices may still be embedded in the education system and how, in particular, these practices work to prevent elementary educators from gaining access to higher levels in their careers. In this context, the similarities and differences in terms of internal, colonial practices and dynamics of inequity across dimensions of class, gender and race would be, in my view, particularly noteworthy and requiring explanation.

According to Tuhiwani Smith cited in Dei & Johal (2005), "[t]o resist is to retrench in the margins, retrieve what we were and remake ourselves. The past, our stories local and global, the present, our communities, cultures, languages and social practices all may be spaces of marginalization, but they may have also become spaces of resistance and hope." Colonialism, racism and gender discrimination are all connected to interlocking systems of hegemonic practices of oppression that I am investigating in both the Ghanaian and Canadian education systems. Being a Canadian born, visible minority female, my personal location gives a sense of hope and added meaning to my study by having shared experience and understanding of the social barriers that exist, as well as striving to build capacity with the existing personal and professional agency with our communities. I will explore the social construction of these dynamics, while also attempting to identify personal attributes and examine the professional actions and acumen that need to be lived on a daily basis in order to attain success. It is important to look at leadership, and understand how to access information from social professional groups. In this sense, the study aspires to balance relevant empirical-theoretical inquiry with my desire to produce an applied outcome tool to support all marginalized educators on an individual and community level.

Multi-Positionality and The Study

The term *visible minority* throughout this study is a central descriptor for racialized groups or *people of colour* within a Canadian context. An *ethnic minority* is a central descriptor for an under-represented ethnicity within the education system such as Ewe and Ga ethnicities. These distinctions express different dynamics, in culturally and historically bounded ways, across the two countries from which I drew my data. In the case of Ghana, for example, I necessarily address the matter of ethnicism: a form of ethnic nationalism, characterized by close identification with other members of the group for whom identity politics is crucial. (Bailey & Gayle, 2003) Generally speaking, the term social difference addresses processes of marginalization affecting groups in terms of gender, socio-economic class, age, disability, ethnic origin, sexuality, etc. For the purposes of this study, the two social difference identities of focus are primarily race and gender understood in culturally specific ways. However, this study and its findings can be meaningful and empowering to all marginalized education professionals. Identity politics brings complexity to the study. The identity politics emerges from an educator's point of *intersectionality*. Identity politics has emerged as a response to challenges by groups of working-class and women of colour to the assumption of *universal woman*. It assumes that cultural, racial/ethnic, and other identities are diverse and that presentation of identity in social life should be determined by those within particular groups, rather than by media representation or some other outside entity. The concept of identity politics is endemic to post-modern societies and is the major focus of feminism and multiculturalism.

Intersectionality is a sociology term that reflects how our various social and cultural identities interact on multiple and often simultaneous levels, contributing to systemic social inequality. We each reflect a cross-section of multiple identities, social differences within society, including race/ethnicity, gender, religion, nationality, sexual orientation, class, or disability that do not act independently of one another.

Philomena Essed (1991), Florence Abena Dolphyne (1991) and Aruna Rao, Rieky Stuart and David Kelleher (1999) suggest structural changes are needed to counter-act the social reproduction process pertaining to race and gender in various social class discussions. However, these authors ideological continuum includes both structural (systemic, institutional or community) and individual empowerment. Will the educational and occupational outcomes have more similar or different patterns of barriers and supports in the Ghanaian and Canadian education systems? What is the relationship between structural forces and cultural innovation? How much autonomy do individuals have at an economic and cultural level, amidst conditions of gendered, racial and class differences? Although the Ghanaian and Canadian contexts are obviously different, such questions are crucial to our understanding of how social inequity is reproduced, and prevents marginalized groups and individuals from gaining access to upward career mobility within an educational work system.

Sketching the Study

Paul Standish cited in Hare and Portelli (2005) state "all research begins with values...to resuscitate a picture of the theory-practice relation ...an understanding of the ethics of education that the humble practitioner can put into operation."

The study attempts to show gaps in the knowledge of the existing research, particularly research on career mobility in educational settings for marginalized groups. I will discuss how my research will contribute to new knowledge. Through the literature, we will explore and assess various conceptual and theoretical issues as a basis for developing a specific theoretical approach to understanding the data. The overarching themes are: career mobility and leadership in education, social difference focusing on race, gender and institutional power, expressed and reproduced through the mutually constituting interaction of multiple forms of what I refer to as *accumulation practices* – i.e. the accumulation of educational or human capital, social capital and cultural capital. These themes are organized to address the historical traces and current values of career mobility, educational leadership, racial and gender scholarship. I choose to see educational leadership themes and challenges through a lens of social difference in order to explore how each social inequity uniquely, yet collectively influenced by various structural conditions.

From a sociological perspective, I am critically analyzing educational workplaces in international contexts to understand how marginalized groups including visible minorities and women are impacted by the limits of the educational work system and in turn may impact such institutions.

> *Bureaucratic insurgency and embedded social barriers in the system creates a feeling of an impenetrable reality for marginalized professionals who are trying to gain promotions in education leadership.*

This research analyzes how the social barriers of race and gender intersectionalities are implicated in school promotion; and how multiple forms of *capital* supports or suppresses career mobility in Ghana and Canada.

> With this in mind, **there are three central research questions that frame the study:**
> 1. What personal attributes and professional navigation actions does one need to be successful in elementary school leadership?
>
> 2. At the institutional level of lived social reality, to what extent do social differences create barriers or enhance the career mobility of elementary school practitioners?
>
> 3. Acknowledging the supports and barriers, what are the multiple, interactive 'capitals' that shape the intersection of career mobility and social differences, and what patterns can be discerned through the comparison of the Ghanaian and Canadian principal promotion process?

Taken as a whole, answers to these three research questions will provide an exploration of the themes emergent from both data sets in terms of career mobility, leadership and social difference representation in the two global education systems. The applied dimension of this research is strongest in my view:

(1) Through the inclusion of my investigation of personal attributes and professional navigational actions that have led to successful progression to positions in education administration.

(2) I combine this discussion of attributes and navigational actions with my analysis of the extent to which social difference and various processes of capital accumulation create barriers or opportunities for the promotion of elementary school practitioners in two cross-cultural contexts.

(3) By the end of the analysis, all of these elements inform my construction of a "Conscious Career Elevation" model which is intended to allow individual practitioners to make better strategic decisions about their career.

It is important to note that there is an agency and structure dialectic that is analyzed throughout this study: specifically, I seek to address the individual, their potential for agency and change located within specific social contexts that I refer to as a *tension field*. For decades, many marginalized groups including visible minorities and women have been overlooked or denied access to key leadership positions and promotional opportunities in education and other fields. This study is designed to identify a standard set of personal and professional attributes which will give concrete navigational tools to aspiring visible minorities and female educators and others trying to find occupational openings for achievement to attain leadership. Yet, the personal agency supported by even the best navigational tools is not enough. We must also understand the social context and the reproductive structure that these aspiring educational leaders face and thus, analyze the dynamic interactions of multiple forms of capital.

The study of career mobility is multi-faceted and complex, thus the in-depth interview narratives and the comparative analysis method are both necessary and appropriate to tackle the complexities of interlocking identities and social difference in the personal experience of leadership and career mobility. The lens of social difference is instrumental in this analysis. It makes sense to also ask, *why this study now?*

This has a three-prong answer:
1. 1.This study informs the current status and problems of representation, access and equity in the educational promotional process.

2. This study extends to the barriers that will be perpetuated to the next generation of marginalized groups including visible minority and female students who are our future educators and principals. Not addressing these matters now, ratifies injustice in the future and the next generation will be burdened by a failure to act.

3. There is general research literature surrounding some of the issues of concern here. The literature highlights some of the problems, but there is still much room left for addressing issues of equity, and for identifying, creating and implementing solutions. Specifically, there is not to my knowledge any relevant "how to" tools for navigating the education system for visible minority groups or marginalized individuals.

Although this study focuses on simply one specific level of one employment sector (the elementary school system) in two specific locations, it may also offer some broader contributions to understanding the career "climb" in broader terms supporting deeper understandings of how career mobility is generated and how leadership attainment relates to minority groups. Some limitations of the study:

(1) Having a limited scope in terms of who I interviewed, educators who became principals. I did not include the perspectives of current or retired teachers, superintendents, parents, and others who I am sure would have provided further insights to or supplemented narratives of current school principals' and their career mobility journey into school administration. This would have been ideal; however, the size of such a broadened approach would have been prohibitive.

(2) At the same time, I would also like to point out that this is by no means an exhaustive study of career mobility in education: it focuses primarily (though not exclusively) on the experiences of minorities. It is premised on the notion of hearing the voices of

marginality. What became clear to me, however, was that these stories are a microcosm of the existing system more broadly, reflecting dominant and minority cultures, men and women, various social class positions, in the sense that any part of the whole, when adequately analyzed, can provide a meaningful means of exploring the whole: in this case the *whole* of at least elementary school career mobility in Ontario, Canada and Koforidua, Ghana.

(3) Finally, as is often the case in research of this kind, directly presenting all the narratives and survey-style data I gathered from my research proved impossible. Space obviously prohibits the full, explicit representation of all the stories of all the respondents. Nevertheless, each and every individual piece of data played a role in shaping the argument I put forth here: some stories emerged as central exemplars of the key dynamics of interest, others served as comparative data and showed variations on a theme, and still others remained in the sub-text as further examples only briefly referenced. In the end, I used material that I thought was relevant to the discussion at hand.

Educators Flowing Through History: Rapids, Waves and Calm Waters

The purpose of studying history is not to deride human action …but to understand it – and then to learn from it as we contemplate our future. (Nelson Mandela cited in Crwys-Williams, 1997) This chapter builds on the *blueprint* of the study. The blueprint is constructed on the knowledge and foundation of epistomological, ontological and ideological premises, as well as historical underpinnings that illuminate its evolution as a research discussion. Both, Koforidua, Ghana and Ontario, Canada have their unique history and struggle in terms of formal education and career mobility. Due to legislation, historical and contemporary government, the Ghanaian education system is under federal jurisdiction. In Canada, the education system is under provincial legislation – in the case of my research, the jurisdiction of Ontario. Thus, the study is informed by the federal education system of Ghana and the provincial education system of Ontario. In addition, this chapter outlines brief past and present accounts of both Ghana and Ontario.

The appreciation of the social and historical factors that will influence career mobility aspirations for elementary school practitioners is significant for the researcher, as well as the reader, to link his or her location to the research objective. This is in order to begin the train of thought connecting each scholar to key issues of promotion. Once one has made this connection, I urge the reader to take a step back. Examine the bigger picture of the pendulum swinging back and forth from matters of social/organizational structures, to personal empowerment and the possibility of transformative action. I argue that understanding the relationship between both of these aspects of reality is how occupational mobility (or lack thereof) of marginalized groups and individuals' works. It is important to keep these questions at the forefront while diving into the history of both nations:

1. How does history inform the current educational promotion issue in both, Koforidua, Ghana and Ontario, Canada?
2. What recurring historical patterns of oppression or domination are experienced that linger in these education systems today?
3. What trends and configurations do we see of social difference and promotion for elementary education practitioners?

Ghanaian Primary (Elementary) Education System

Ghana is a former British colony known as Gold Coast before it gained its independence in 1957. It was the first Sub-Saharan country to gain independence. There are more than 100 languages and dialects spoken in Ghana. However, English is the official language. Cultures also vary from region to region. Ghanaian's education history is divided into two parts: pre-colonial *informal* education and Western education. *Informal education* or types of informal apprenticeship was the dominant mode of transmitting knowledge in pre-colonial societies. Proper roles and behaviours were learned by observing adults, actively doing, and supported more broadly through the production and transmittance of proverbs, folktales and songs. Intense moral instruction was developed at various stages of life, especially during puberty rites. Religion or spirituality was also included in the *curriculum*. (UNESCO, 2007; Buah, 1998)

Western education influence was:

1. Initialized as early as 1765 and introduced in the southern regions of Ghana by Presbyterian and Methodist missionaries. Some Western merchants also played a role in introducing Western education.

2. In 1957, Ghana's independence came with many educational reforms, including free and compulsory primary education. At this time, the government took over the management of schools. The country had only one university and a few secondary schools at independence. Policy solidified free and compulsory education for junior secondary (middle school) in 1961 through the introduction of the Education Act.

3. In 1966, the overthrow of President Kwame Nkrumah began the formation of the Education Review Committee which re-introduced education cost-sharing between the parents and the government.

4. The government in 1979 created the Constitution of the Third Republic in which, free and compulsory primary education was revived and it was extended to secondary education subject to availability of funds.

5. However, in the 1980s, Ghana's education system was in crisis. Existing policies could not be implemented due to the financial crisis facing Ghana at the time. In 1985, half of the country's primary and middle school teachers were untrained. Primary attrition rate stood at 60%. In 1987, Ghana reduced pre-tertiary years from 17 to 12: 6 years primary; 3 junior secondary; 3 years senior secondary and 4 years tertiary.

The Indigenous languages became the medium of instruction in the early years of primary education. (UNESCO, 2007; Ghana Education Paper from CIA, 2006) The financial crisis in the Ghanaian education system impacted the students and teachers.

However, in terms of this study, we can also ask: how the forces of history have influenced teachers and their careers? In terms of career mobility and teacher development in Ghana comparatively from the past to today, there is more opportunity for job rotation, specializing in a particular grade.

Typically, there is only one head primary teacher, yet there are teacher subject specialists. In late 1990s, there was a one year reduction in Teacher Training Education in Ghana. Under the Education Reform Program, the program has changed from a 4-year program to a 3-year program. Akyeampong (2003) argued that "there is a total lack of commitment by the education establishment to the early years of the beginning teachers' professional life. Three years spent in formal training does not produce the kind of changes expected or necessary for effective teaching." This did not only affect the quality of their training, overall skills and knowledge-base and credentials received, but in terms of promotion (Dei, 2006), some teachers were at a disadvantage unless their years of experience or teacher leadership were supported in their promotional process. For example, Collins' (1979) credentialing argument implies that mobilized professional and managerial employees with *specialized knowledge claims* will generally be sufficiently successful in restricting access to educational credentials, and that there will be little difference between their actual attainments and the credential requirements determined necessary for future career opportunities. Thus, Collins argues that one year less of teacher training would not make much of a difference on the job, or for promotional purposes, due to the fact that *specialized knowledge claims* or *experiential knowledge* are attained primarily with job-embedded learning. In the case of Ghana, these types of findings raise important questions about the nature of career mobility.

Yaw Osafo-Maafo, former Minister of Education states "the Ministry of Education and Sports exists to carry out the Government's vision of using quality education delivery to accelerate the nation's socio economic development." (Ghanaian Ministry of Education, 2006) Ghana since independence made significant strides in its education system. The education landscape in Ghana today is the result of major policy initiatives in education, adopted by past governments as well as the present one. Indeed these initiatives have not only helped in structurally transforming the education system, but also have improved access, quality of teaching and learning, infrastructure delivery and management efficiency.

Some of the laws, policy documents and reports which have helped in meeting the educational needs and aspirations of the people are:
- The Education Act of 1961
- The Dzobo Report of 1973 (Recommended the JSS Concept)
- The New Structure and Content of Education 1974
- The Education Commission Report on Basic and Secondary Education 1987/88

- The University Relationalization Committee Report 1988
- The Ghana Education Trust Fund - GET Fund Act 2000 (Act 581)

These additional policy mandates were designed to address some of the shortcomings of these educational reforms:

- *The Education Reform Program 1987/88 and the Free Compulsory Universal Basic Education Program, 1996 (1992 Constitution):* Have contributed immensely to the structure of Basic Education that Ghana has today and the achievements made. Basic Education now consists of 6 years Primary Education followed by 3 years Junior Secondary. (Ghanaian Ministry of Education, 2006).

- *The Quality Improvement in Primary Schools (QUIPS) Program:* Supported by USAID, among other elements, helps to produce competent teachers, train education managers and planners and promote a supportive learning environment.

- *The Child School Community Progress in Education (Child Scope) is a UNICEF sponsored program:* Helps to improve children's reading, writing and numeracy skills in primary schools.

- *The District Teacher Support Team (DSTS):* Provides an anchor for improving the quality of teaching and learning at the district level. It provides support to schools in the area of good practices in literacy, numeracy and problem solving.

- *The Whole School Development (WSD) program:* Is a GES strategy for mainstreaming all interventions for the achievements of the FCUBE objectives. Zone co-coordinators have been appointed to serve as a link between pre-service and in-service teacher education programs. They also link District and Regional management personnel to Teacher Training Colleges. In addition to Teacher Training Colleges, zone co-coordination, pre-service and in-service programs and teachers, there are other new innovative and technologically-mediated ways teacher's can advance their skills and knowledge-base to be competitive for career mobility. First, there are Information Communications Technology (ICT) Education and Distance Learning available for teachers to upgrade their skills. Second, the Decentralization and Community Participation program and the Functional Literacy Program both give exposure to teaching and school program methods in rural and urban areas for school partnership, network and growth. Finally, the Presidential Review Committee on Education and the Education Sector Review Committee has initiated a program called The Way Forward; it is a Quality Education Initiative for the classroom and for their professional development.

Policies of the Ghanaian primary school system indicate that educators must exhibit exemplary teaching performance in the following areas:

i)   numeracy and literacy

ii) laying the foundation for inquiry and creativity;

iii) development of sound moral attitudes and a healthy appreciation of Ghana's cultural heritage and identity;

iv) development of the ability to adapt constructively to a changing environment;

v)   laying the foundation for the development of manipulative and life skills that will prepare the individual pupils to function effectively to their own advantage as well as that of their community;

vi) inculcating good citizenship education as a basis for effective participation in national development.

vii) incorporating in daily lessons the revised national curriculum comprising the following subjects for all Primary Schools are: Mathematics, Science, Social Studies, Cultural Studies, Ghanaian Languages, English, Agriculture, Life Skills and Physical Education. (UNESCO, 2006; The World Factbook, 2006; Ghana's Ministry of Education, 2006)

Ghanaian primary or elementary practitioners' aspiring to be an elementary school administrator has a multiplicity of ways to gain access to professional development. Some pathways incur financial expense, which may limit some options such as distance learning and attending the Information Technology Centres. However, the majority of the professional development programs are operated by non-government organizations such as UNICEF, or multilateral global organizations including the International Monetary Fund (IMF) and the World Bank. There are other professional development programs that are fully or partially subsidized by the Ghanaian government. Moreover, it is important to note that there are economic disparities affecting teacher professional development. What seems clear is that the rise of professional colleges and distance education-learning centres changed the face of Ghanaian educational accrual. Enrolment rates in such programs improved as did the use of information technology. However, the unevenness of access to human capital investment and professional credentials for educators has produced an *opportunity gap* for elementary practitioners' skills and promotional attainment that affect teachers differentially.

In Ghanaian data, the preliminary background information tells us that the main language is English and there are many ethnic secondary languages such as Twi-Ashanti and Akwapim, Ewe and Ga. The interviews were conducted in English; however, I had a local bilingual translator for a few interviews due to communication barriers. There were six male respondents and nine female respondents. The ethnic origins ranged from Twi (Ashanti/Akwapim), Ga and Ewe. Many schools were located in sub-urban areas; however, some considered rural from Western perspective, in terms of resources such as no electricity and running water. The age range was 36-60. The years of experience as a school administrator were three years and higher. All principals and teachers were unionized under an umbrella organization. All elementary schools and their principals had religious affiliations. The education level ranged from O-Level (Equivalent Grade 12 High School) to a Bachelor degree. The Ghanaian Education Service has a thirteen step ranking process in educational promotion.

Ghanaian Education Promotion Policies from the Ministry
PLACEMENT OF TEACHING STAFF

1. **Certificate "A"** 3 years Post Secondary
2. **Superintendent II** – After four (4) years of service, Inspection of practical teaching and record of work.
3. **Superintendent I** – promotion by interview after four (4) years of service.
4. **Senior Superintendent II** – promotion by interview after three (3) years of Service
5. **Senior Superintendent I** – promotion by interview after three (3) years of Service
6. **Principal Superintendent** – promotion by interview after 4 – 5 years at Regional level
7. **Assistant Director II** – promotion by interview at National Headquarters after three (3) years service.
8. **Assistant Director I** - promotion by interview at National Headquarters after three (3) years service

---

9. **Deputy Director** – promotion by interview at National level by Education Service Council after three (3) or more years.

10. **Director II** - promotion by interview at National level by Education Service Council after three (3) or more years.

11. **Director 1** - promotion by interview at National level by Education Service Council after three (3) or more years.

12. **Deputy Director General** - Political appointment on recommendation by Education Service Council for consideration by government in power.

13. **Director General** – Purely Political and on the recommendation by the Education Service Council.

NB: The highest rank for non-graduate teachers is Assistant Director I. The Positions from Deputy Director to the Director General is reserved for first and second Degree holders.

IMPLEMENTATION OF THE RECOMMENDED SCHEME OF SERVICE FOR PERSONNEL IN THE GHANA EDUCATION SERVICE

Canadian/Ontarian Elementary Education System

The ancestors of the First Nations have inhabited parts of what is now called Canada since the retreat of glaciers that marked the end of the last ice age. Archaeological records show that these lands have been inhabited for at least 10,000 years. Several Viking expeditions occurred circa AD 1000, with evidence of settlement at L'Anse aux Meadows (The World Factbook, 2006). When the British and French colonized thereafter, they established a school system which attempted to *separate* public and religious schools in Canada. In 1841, the Legislature of Canada East and Canada West were created. Since about half of the members of the Legislature were French Canadian Catholics, they enacted the first piece of separate school legislation. In 1867 section 93(1) of the *British North America Act* guaranteed in perpetuity these rights. The *Separate* school historical struggle to be autonomous and receive funding from the government equal to that of the Public School Board has been long standing. The financial implications of this religious or *separate* and public elementary school boards' disagreement escalated when the financial demands on the education system rose in the catastrophic Great Depression (1929-1939).

The Great Depression had serious financial, political and systemic impacts on education. The Great Depression caused Canada, economic turmoil and disorder which lead to increased stratification in the decentralized provincial system. This caused Canada to re-build the funding base, curriculum, school administration, structure, and many other aspects of education.

Since then, the Canadian, and specifically the Ontario school system has made many changes in elementary schools. My comments here, as above in terms of Ghana, merely attempt to provide a basic understanding of some key historical elements which would attempt to explain how elementary education works. Canada's provincial governance of elementary schools' cover:

(1) decision making for public schools (roles and responsibilities of provincial, local, and federal governments);

(2) paying for public education (revenue sources and allocation, public funding of *separate* religious schools, summaries of governance and finance for each province);

(3) requirements to address the needs of students, bilingual education, language instruction for immigrant students, education for Native children, and others;

(4) cooperative, distance and international education;

(5) financial support and institutional funding, tax supports;

(6) teachers in the workforce, gender issues in the teaching profession and teacher education, and others.

The historical trends in the Canadian elementary school system until recent contemporary times; have focused on curriculum outcomes and assessment as opposed to equity in schools on a provincial level.

To advance the expansion of education policy, Kathleen Wynne, former Ontario Minister of Education, led the way in the creation of Ontario's Equity and Inclusive Policy/Program Memorandum 119. Having registered the provincial policies, curriculum, accountability, quality and school administrative mandates, we can now ask: what are the economic supports available in the maintenance and implementation process? After finding out how the Ministry of Education funds the provincial initiatives, school administration can look into partnership policies, curriculum policies and mandates, to succeed in practice and promotion within Ontario that would reinforce the goal of ensuring quality and accountability. An elementary school practitioner who aspires to understand and navigate the system needs to know and practice the following Ontario Ministry of Education and Ontario College of Teachers (OCT) policies:

- Education Act and Teacher Professionalism
- Guidelines for Policy Development and Implementation, Antiracism and Ethno-cultural Equity in School Boards (1993)
- Bill 31, Ontario College of Teachers (1996)
- Bill 160, Education Quality Improvement Act (1997)
- PPM 119, Equity and Inclusive Education Strategy (2009 replaced 1993)
- Bill 168, Workplace Violence and Harassment (2010)
- The Standards of Practice for the Teaching Profession (OCT, 2006)
- The Ethical Standards for the Teaching Profession (OCT, 2006)

These Acts complement the promotional process. However, an elementary educator who is intentionally looking for a future administrative position must "be both masters of research-based pedagogical technique, and capable of personal charismatic, creative and imaginative engagement… education is a matter of improving people in some substantial normative sense." (Portelli & Hare, 2005) David Carr cited in Portelli & Hare (2005) believes that a master teacher is a moral, technical and artistic matter of improving the school community. This is indicative of an individual's competence level in her school community, however, it is essential that an aspiring elementary school educator understands her role as an individual within the system and how the system also affects the school community. This understanding is key to self-agency which translates to systemic reform and moving forward in the acceptance of social difference.

In Canadian data, the preliminary background information tells us that the main language is English and French. There were seven male respondents and eight female respondents. There are many ethnicities represented, their origin or descent ranged some included European, African, West Indian, and Chinese. The schools were located in sub-urban areas; however, some were in residential areas and some were in urban lower-income areas. The age range was 35-65. The years of experience as a school administrator were one year and higher. Both teachers were unionized and the principals are not in Ontario. The sample had half from the Public school board and half from the Catholic school board. The principals education level ranged from Bachelor degree with two specialists to Masters degree with specialist certification.

It is important to note, the formalized Ontario Ministry of Education promotional process from elementary school teacher to Director of Education:

Ontario's Promotional Process- From Elementary Teacher to Director of Education

1. Certified Teacher with Ontario College of Teachers
2. Attain five to seven years of successful teaching experience
3. Have a Master's or two specialist certifications
4. Take Principal Qualification Program Part I and II, and attain some successful years as a vice principal to apply for Principal.
5. After having successful years in several principalships, principals take Superintendent course
6. Apply for position of superintendent, after that Director of Education of a School Board which Doctoral degree is desired but not required

*Different school boards have different selection criteria, processes, and timelines. Possible to stay unilaterally at each stage.

There is more fluidity and open-ended decision-making to move forward in Canada than in Ghana. It is important to maintain boundaries and to want to change a piece of the education system puzzle. This system transformation could be initiated through *self-referential system* or observing the functions (Luhman, 2006). Unlike Zimmermann's (2004) approach to system transformation stating "as a substitution of previous fundamental political and economic institutions in a polity by new (or different) political and economic institutions." Canadian occupational or career mobility determinants are rooted on the individual, school, community and education system levels; general points which I will begin to address in the next section.

Structuring the Flow of the Study

Merriam & Simpson (2000) states "when we are doing research, we are committed to systematically searching the breadth and/or depth of a situation or phenomenon, often from numerous vantage points." The purpose of this section is to provide an outline of how the study was conducted.

I understand the study as akin to the comments by Merriam and Simpson (2000) when they described research as "the process of re-search systematically looking at a situation or phenomenon, not occasionally or causally, but again and again until certain previously stated criteria, goals, or guidelines of inquiry are met." Below I discuss the following information:

(1) The type of data used and reasons for their use;
(2) The way in which the interviewees were selected;
(3) How the data was analyzed after being collected;
(4) Precautions I had to take as the researcher to ensure that the data and its analysis will justify inferences drawn from them.

The research procedures were designed to apply a series of specific concepts and theories to uncover the complexity of the practical realities of aspiring educators, attempting to advance their careers from teacher to school principal in elementary education systems in Ghana and Canada. The study of career mobility is multi-faceted and complex. Thus, the in-depth interview narratives and comparative analysis methods are both necessary and appropriate to tackle the complexities of *interlocking identities* and differences in the personal experience of career mobility. Here I discuss the usefulness of a qualitative methodological approach, how I used the interviewee narratives. I would like to make a point of clarification that the narrative group throughout this study is synonymous with an interview group and should be read as such. For analyzing and interpreting the data, I targeted commonalities or emerging themes as well as marked differences while also drawing on observations from the field and my own experience as a Canadian as well as an international educator.

Using this methodology design as a guide for the following questions:

1. What is the sample size and its implications? What is the basis for comparability across different national contexts?

2. Seeing that methodology reflects the researchers experience, what precautions does a researcher need to take in analyzing her data?

3. How can the researcher take into account cross-cultural variables when conducting and analyzing the results of the data?

There are three main sections in the data collection:

Data Collection Method

Triangulation Data Collection

Observation and Reflective Notes | Preliminary Survey-Style Questions | Semi-Structured Interviews

The use of the multi-method approach lends itself to particular windows of knowledge and comparison of methodological approaches. I think that having the qualitative component, hearing the stories, voices, struggle and pain of the promotion process as well as the lack of access to it could only be illuminated in an interview format. As the researcher, I had insights to their personal and professional accounts of leadership, failures, successes and love for education. The narrative or interview style of acquiring information connects you to the experience and life history of a person that just couldn't be reached in quantitative research. However, the survey-styled data helped to hone in on certain themes in the research that needed that binary element to it. The survey-styled data was the background support or validation to the narratives or interviews. Moreover, the triangular nature of the study was a necessary lesson: the interviews, the survey-styled questions as well as having key observations and noting challenges that the researcher experienced. The second section considers a discussion of the research sample, recruitment process, and data collection methods. Further, it discusses the analysis and interpretation of the data, and finally, the validity of the data. Under each section, I will comparatively discuss both Canada and Ghana as they relate to the theme of the section and oscillate between converging and diverging themes.

In general, I offered an invitation for consultation on career issues which began with subjects filling out data with survey-style questions after which I conducted in-depth interviews to gather further information. There is a distinction between *sources* of data (people) and forms of data collection (from the same person). My data is based on people's stories or narratives supplemented by objective questions that allow some basic claims regarding comparability. "The use of multiple sources of data for qualitative research is called triangulation, which increases the reliability of the research, and allows data to be compared and confirmed in more than one way." (Dei, 2005; Foster, 1990) A form of triangulation is possible through my attention to text analysis, critical observation, interviews and comparing data from survey-styled questions. This study's methodological approach is in line with Foster's comments (1990) that, "...effective research allows participants to formulate their own answers through open-ended interviews. Though more time consuming, such interviews encourage subjects to express feelings and ideas in their own words, resulting in more in-depth accounts."

Hearing the Voice of Principals through Data

The data sources were varied in terms of racial/ethnic origin, gender, age, class and were looked at in a national and international context. The situation was set-up so as to generate at least some observational data: in some instances, elementary school administrators were observed in their professional environment providing additional context, background and preparation for effective in-depth interviews as well as data analysis. Building on the notion of *triangulation*, as Lather (1986) says, "[w]hat is noteworthy in the triangulation process is how concrete situations influenced theory-building and proceeded in a manner that fostered the participants' awareness of their own resources and their right to influence decisions concerning themselves." Perhaps, I hoped, this research design would serve to *empower* educators. (Freire, 1971; Troyna, 1994)

The critical awareness informing this project starts with the initial engagement with the politics of difference (Bulmer & Solomos, 2004). While race is salient, the *intersections* of gender and other social differences influence and limit the social and career mobility opportunities within the elementary school system as well.

> *The scope of marginality depends upon the education systems' readiness to address the politics of difference.*

Critical awareness of racial constructions and the social factors influencing *racial engagement for oppression and liberation* are necessary to raise and answer significant questions about power, influence, mobilization, agency and resistance. As one way of seeing, critical awareness offers inclusive approaches to the politics, accessibility, professional development and new possibilities in professional partnerships. These issues have methodological implications. This study does not pretend to be a universal remedy in response to the systemic inequalities is often evident in the elementary education system's promotional procedures. This is an attempt to identify common navigational tools that could assist marginalized groups or individuals to empower themselves or to gain awareness of the multiple barriers politically, socially, economically and culturally that present themselves daily. In other words, as a qualitative research project with hopes that what I have produced will have applied value for practitioners, I would like this study to serve as a reflective tool, for the participants by individually sharing their discoveries with those being studied. (Dei & Johal, 2005) This, in turn, has shaped my choice of subjects, the type of data I chose to collect, as well as the specific questions I asked.

I started the recruitment of participants for the study in mid-June 2006. I wanted the sample size to be an accurate reflection of the school boards demographic in both Canada and Ghana, in terms of race, gender, class, age, religion and various ethnic representations. Additionally, the participants all had official principal certifications from their school policies or ministry mandates, and held a position of principal or head master or mistress in an elementary school. The study entailed gathering data at two different municipal sites representing important regional and organizational variation: Ontario, Canada (medium sized suburban/

urban, Public and Catholic School Boards) and Koforidua, Ghana (small mixed suburban/rural, Elementary Schools Unit). In total, there were two individual research sites representing the key spheres of activity.

In order to fully grasp the range of learning activities and to completely contextualize those activities in the complex organizational setting in which they occurred, an in-depth interview approach was required to collect the data. Participants of varying years of service, educational experience, and ethno-cultural affiliations were sought to create a sample base of fifteen principals in each country. The total number of respondents (principals) in the data set was 30, 15 from Ghana and 15 from Canada. Participants were selected based on the following information: currently employed as an associate, vice principal or principal of an elementary school, a consenting adult, and a willingness to participate in the study.

SURVEY QUESTIONS
Elementary School Administrators
Survey- Introduction Question

As an educator, could you rank from 1 to 10 the most important attribute in career mobility within your organization or education system?

_____ Higher Education
_____ Superior Job Performance
_____ Personal Style
_____ High Visibility Assignment
_____ Influential Mentors
_____ Political Astuteness
_____ Seniority/Experience
_____ Good Relationship with Management
_____ Creativity and Innovations Added To Your Organization
_____ International Experience

Survey-Part I
Leadership, Politics and Organizational Culture

1. By what percentage does seeking out difficult or high visibility assignments assist your move towards upward mobility?
   _____ 100%-81% _____ 80%-61% _____ 60%-41%
   _____ 40%-21% _____ 20%- 0%

2. Do you have a strategy for your career advancement?
   _____ Yes   _____ No

   If yes, have you begun its implementation?
   _____ High Degree
   _____ Fair/Adequate
   _____ Not at All

   If yes, does your strategy have a timeline?
   _____ Yes   _____ No

3. Do you think having a mentor would assist you in terms of structure and knowledge within your organization towards advancement?
   _____ Yes   _____ No

   Do you have a mentor?
   _____ Yes   _____ No

4. Is there the presence of an informal network in your organizational group setting?
   _____ Yes   _____ No

   Does this informal network have influence on decision making powers in your organization?
   _____ Yes   _____ No

   If yes, to what degree?
   _____ 100%-81% _____ 80%-61% _____ 60%-41%
   _____ 40%-21% _____ 20%- 0%

5. Which do you think cross-functional job rotation or specializing in a particular job and skill set would assist more in terms of advancement? Please choose one only.
   _____ Cross-Functional Job Rotation   _____ Specializing

What three characteristics merit superior job performance? Please prioritize by number 1 being the most important and number 5 being the least)

_____ Dedication (requires after hours work)

_____ Accuracy (on daily tasks)

_____ Punctuality   _____ Consistency

_____ Extra-Curricular Activities

_____ Other (if other, please list the characteristic _____)

6. How much do you think personality factors into advancement?

_____ 100%-81% _____ 80%-61% _____ 60%-41%

_____ 40%-21% _____ 20%- 0%

7. Who do you think is accountable for your career development?

_____ Management

_____ Mentor

_____ Yourself

_____ Other (if possible, please write down the specific role.)

8. Are specific academic qualifications necessary for your advancement in your organization?

_____ Yes   _____ No

What kind of degree do you need to attain a top management position?

_____ B.A. _____ M. Ed. _____ M.A. _____ Ph. D _____ Ed. D

_____ Post Ph. D

9. What kind of system does your organization generally operate on a merit-based, performance-based or on a seniority (the number of years an employee accumulates in their respective organization)?

_____ Merit-based _____ Performance-based

_____ Seniority

Is there a reward system in place to reinforce seniority?

_____ Yes   _____ No

Do you have to obtain a certain amount or number of years of experience to advance in your organization?

_____ Yes   _____ No

If yes, how many years on average does it take to advance from one position to a higher one?

_____ 0-1 year _____ 1-2 years _____ 3-5 years _____ 6-7 years

_____ 7-10 years

10. Would creation or innovation add value to your organization?
   _____ Yes   _____ No
   How much do you think creation and innovation would contribute to your career development?
   _____ 100%-81% _____ 80%-61% _____ 60%-41%
   _____ 40%-21% _____ 20%- 0%

11. What is the key factor to maintaining a good relation with your superior?
   _____ Integrity   _____ Accountability
   _____ Effective Listener   _____ Encouraging
   _____ Initiative   _____ Work Stamina
   _____ Open Communication   _____ Team Builder
   _____ Good Conflict   _____ Supportive
   _____ Competence Resolution Skills   _____ Other
   (Please List, the Key Factor (_____)

12. Does the exposure that international experience brings assist in career development?
   _____ Yes   _____ No
   If yes, what kind of experience is merited?
   _____ Vacations   _____ Summer Work Abroad
   _____ Living/Working Abroad   _____ Student Exchange
   _____ International Conferences   _____ Teacher Exchange

Survey- Part II
Social Difference

13. Do you think race or ethnicity is a factor that could prohibit someone from gaining access to promotion? How so, explain _____
   _____
   _____ Yes   _____ No

14. What percentage of cross-cultural vice or associate principals do you have within your School Board? Could you briefly describe your nationality? _____
   _____ 100%-81% _____ 80%-61% _____ 60%-41%
   _____ 40%-21% _____ 20%- 0%

15. What percentage of other ethnic/racial principals do you have within your School Board?

_____ 100%-81% _____ 80%-61% _____ 60%-41%
_____ 40%-21% _____ 20%- 0%

16. In your view, is there a racial hierarchy of acceptance within your School Board?

_____ Yes _____ No

If so, what races are at the top of the hierarchy? _____
_____
_____

17. Are there informal networks between certain other ethnic/racial communities?

_____ Yes _____ No

18. Are there informal networks between dominant groups?

_____ Yes _____ No

19. If yes to Question 18 or 19, do these informal networks pass on pertinent information to attain access for promotion or give leadership advice? If yes, what kind of information?

_____ Yes _____ No

Information _____
_____
_____
_____

20. Do you think the dominant group assists the other ethnic/racial groups in attaining access and supports their motivation to become an administrator?

_____ Yes _____ No

21. What percentage of female vice or associate principals do you have within your School Board?

_____ 100%-81% _____ 80%-61% _____ 60%-41%
_____ 40%-21% _____ 20%- 0%

22. What percentage of female principals do you have within your School Board?

_____ 100%-81% _____ 80%-61% _____ 60%-41%
_____ 40%-21% _____ 20%- 0%

23. Are there informal networks or associations between females within your school or your school board?

_____ Yes _____ No

24. Are there informal networks or associations between dominant female groups?

_____ Yes _____ No

25. Are there informal networks or associations for other ethnic/racial female educators?

_____ Yes _____ No

26. In your experience, do you feel women support other women in their career mobility aspirations?

_____ Yes _____ No

27. Are there stigmatism to a person's place of residence or the area that they are from?

_____ Yes _____ No

28. In your view, is a person's social status or background a factor when being considered for an elementary school position?

_____ Yes _____ No

29. Does economic status help or hinder career mobility?

_____ Yes _____ No

30. Do you think a person's cultural capital (skills, credentials, knowledge-base) is considered in promotion?

_____ Yes _____ No

In Ghana, participants were recruited based on public information at the school board principal meetings, in schools, or, by the expression of interest in response from the recruitment letter. To do any work in the village or township, it was customary to greet all of the townspeople and the Chief before conducting research. After a welcoming drumming ceremony, gift exchanges and sharing traditional Ghanaian foods; a cordial partnership was formed and I was given permission to conduct my research. All elementary schools had religious affiliation, and the distances between the schools were quite extensive. Walking on foot in the heat was one source of delay, and the other was a mandatory emergency principal's meeting on a community project, which required me to do some rescheduling to get interviews. In all, the recruitment and interviewing process in Ghana was a source of learning in itself. In Canada, all participants in this study were affiliated with Ontario school boards. Some of the principals had held positions such as head resource teacher, secondary school principals, union leadership positions, school board leadership positions and some were business managers before they gained access to their current leadership position as elementary school principals.

Above are the actual survey-styled questions, and below are the in-depth interview questions. It is a benefit to the reader to take time and complete the survey as well as the interview questions to gauge your own perspective, lens and entry point into the work of career mobility, leadership and social difference. Use yourself as text to explore your positions, privilege, understanding of relational dynamics and networks, and take account of your own accrual of human, social and cultural capital. This will further inform you of the study and anticipation of the participant responses but can also be used as a discussion piece in your current workplace or help with your career planning and navigation strategies to promotion.

INTERVIEW QUESTIONS
Based on Preliminary Survey
Elementary School Administrators

1. a) What qualifications were required and what extra qualifications did you feel you had to attain to compete for the position?
   b) When you interviewed for your administrative position, what preparation did you undertake?
   c) What was the timeframe of your application, interview and response time?

2. In your aspirations to become an elementary school principal, did you create long-term and/or short-term plans? If so, describe them.

3. In your organization, what do you think are the valued characteristics in a potential principal and why?

4. What kind of changes would you like to see in the application and/or interview procedure for elementary school principals within your organization or school board?

5. In your experience, what degree of involvement do you need to have on a school, community and school board level to become a principal?

6. In your view, does seniority play a role for promotional access?

7. Are there policies in place within your organization or school board that you are aware of that ensure other ethnic/racial communities, women and working-class candidates have an equitable application and interview process?

8. In your opinion, do you think other ethnic/racial educators have to work harder and attain higher levels of qualifications to compete for administrative positions? If so, explain.

9. Do you think nepotism exists within your organization in the hiring and career mobility process? Explain.

10. a) Do you think women plan differently from their male counterparts in career mobility? If so, could you describe how this is done?

    b) Do personal circumstances such as women taking time off for maternity to have a family valued in your organization or is it seen as an impediment for your career promotional process? Explain.

11. Is a candidate for an administrative position's address and/or economic status considered? Explain.

12. What are the economic or financial implications for elementary educators who aspire to be a principal? Specifically, do you think an educator of a middle-class or upper-class background has more of an opportunity to succeed as a principal candidate? Why or why not?

13. How many years does a principal have before retirement, what is the year range?

14. In your opinion, what tends to distinguish a candidate from the rest?

15. If you had to choose one of these a ladder, a spiral or a web, which one best describes your career progression?

16. Is horizontal career mobility (an educator promoted to specialized educator position) a valued way of thinking about a career? Why or why not?

17. In your experience, what do you need to have to maintain social mobility and respect when you are a principal?

18. Do you think it is important for you to have the same values as your organization or do you think it is necessary to have value clashes in order for you, your constituents and your organization to grow? Explain and give an example.

19. Have informal networks worked for you or against you as an elementary school principal? Explain.

20. a) What kind of structural changes is necessary to ensure equitable practices for promotional opportunities within your organization?

    b) How does school board culture affect promotion process?

There were some ethical considerations that arose from this study. The first consideration was that there is a question of authenticity when asking the participants about their value system around social difference, leadership and career mobility, what is merited and how they are socially and systemically influenced. As has been noted by scholars, "the education system [has a strong role] in the reproduction of social relations or validity of the concept of meritocracy and the question of who decides which educational knowledge is to be valued and rewarded and which is not" (Troyna, 1994). Unlike so much classic sociology of education literature such as the works of Bernstein (1971) and Bourdieu (1973), amongst others, who have offered extensive analysis show that the reproduction of social inequalities take place. I have sought to include the social difference of race and gender in various social classes, and furthermore to focus on the school as reproductive of social inequities in terms of teachers careers. Foster's (1990) equal opportunities can be based upon *universalistic values of society*. Foster's discussion of *neutrality* of the educational system as arbiter of rewards as well as the 'education for a non-racist society' raises the importance that the universalistic values emulate those of the dominant group can be seen as no coincidence (Connolly, 1992). Can some of the participants acknowledge their power or privilege or does prudence in organizational politics prevail?

Glaser and Strauss conceptualized how the *grounded theory* bridges the gap between empirical and theoretical research; this was the second ethical consideration. Critical awareness and engagement occur through a learning practice of being "grounded" that leads to finding out the phenomena and gaps within the study. Grounded theory procedures force us to ask what power is in this situation, use some *interpretative work* under what specified conditions?" (Strauss & Corbin, 1994) Grounded theory researchers are interested in rational knowledge and patterns of action and interaction between and among various types of social units. "Rational knowledge is a process of ongoing critical interpretation among *fields* of interpreters and decoders." (Donna Haraway cited in Fine & Vanderslice, 1991) Critical reflections and being mindful of the subjects in conversations or critiques will give multiple perspectives as well as overriding themes will emerge. During both Ghanaian and Canadian interviews, I assigned a pseudonym to sustain the anonymity of each participant. The thirty respondents used oral narrative to relate life histories can be quite small (Goodson and Sikes, 2001).

These sample groups of thirty elementary school principals or head masters/mistresses from both Ghana and Canada were sufficient for extrapolating support, understanding the barriers and honing in on the ideologies surrounding social difference, leadership and career mobility aspirations for elementary school practitioners. I categorized the respondents' cross-sectional characteristics of ethnicity, gender, age, years of experience and qualifications earned; this was a form of *descriptive data* gathering. Merriam and Simpson (2000) understand that researchers who explore descriptive research know the importance of selected or sampled data. It was clear that taking initial descriptive information helped to gain insight into the positionality of the respondents. It became evident that some inherit differences and similarities were present in all the respondents in Ghana, for all the principals had religious affiliations, they were all homogeneous in terms of race but experienced divergent ethnic politics manifest in different ethnicities.

Similarly in Canada, principals were either experiencing different forms of the politics of privilege, full career acceptance or denial. Due to the complexities of identity, all the participants represented a selection of different class, age and backgrounds which presented a richer perspective for investigating social difference implications in both the Ghanaian and Canadian contexts. All participants had a post-secondary education, many had a Bachelor and Master degrees. Four of the Ghanaian respondents had Bachelor degrees and many reported financial difficulties and barriers to attaining higher education degrees, while Catholic principals in Ontario could not attain a principalship without achieving a Masters degree or being enrolled in the program.

<u>Research Challenges and Possibilities</u>

There were some challenges to this study:

(1) There were 15 respondents from both Ghana and Canada from a sub-urban municipal area. However, sub-urban municipal areas have vast differences in terms of infrastructure and natural resources, financial resources and education materials. Additionally, the numbers of pupils in the schools in the respective area were notably larger in Ghana. Consequently, some of the differences revealed in this study are important distinctions between rural and sub-urban school principals. For example, the barriers rural principals face on the job were significant, though the interviews nevertheless showed that it was easier to be promoted in a rural school than in a sub-urban, Ontario school. In Koforidua, Ghana, there were other suburban non-religious affiliated public or private school principals that were not reflected in the sample due to the predominant religious affiliated school connections of the interview organizer and proximal distance-transportation issues.

(2) Being of Trinidadian-Canadian descent, it is possible that my Western and Caribbean views may have influenced the participants just by my representation of my body and what it means to be in the places and spaces that I engaged in this research.

(3) In Ghana, ethnic language and origin is an important difference which has power implications. Ghanaians are sometimes perceived as a homogeneous group, however, I think it is important to note that I had 2 Ga participants, 1 Ga and Ewe mixed-origin, 1 Ga and Twi mixed-origin which created the minority voice. The other 11 Twi respondents were the majority voice. Consequently, the mixed-origin ethnic principals did not want to recognize that they were a minority; minority meant a separation from their Akan [Twi-Ashanti and Akwapim] brother and sisters.

(4) In Canada, I focused on publicly-funded school systems thus, there were no private school principals represented.

(5) The minority voices within this Canadian data were few; in part an expression of the under-representation of minority voices in Ontario's educational leadership in general. Those minority principals, who were interviewed, however, offered detailed information, and a careful analysis of majority voices still allowed a critical assessment of career mobility. There were many minority

cultures that were not represented in the sample. Although the notion of multiculturalism is well known in Canadian school boards, the questions attempted to look beyond the status quo and rhetoric to tease out practices and structures of privilege, colorblindness, race and racism in promotion.

(6) The subject matter became too intense for some interviewees and they resisted full engagement with questions along these lines.

(7) The fifteen data sample of principals is an attempt to create a microcosm of the existing system, hearing the voice of the privilege and the few minorities. The complexity of the politics of difference often surfaced in the interviews in other ways as well. For example, one interviewee concluded that the school board did not discriminate in general on the basis of the interviewee's own diagnosed deafness. If the board didn't discriminate in this situation, surely it does not discriminate towards any other group such as race or visible minorities, women, working-class and others. Forms of logical fallacy and contradictions as well as conflation of different forms of social differentiation with each other were something that emerged in interviews both implicitly and explicitly. Moreover, five respondents did not answer some of the survey-styled questions around race, but did not hesitate on other differences such as gender or class. This pitfall in the research helped me to reveal some salient tensions around race and ethnicity around promotion; it is almost taboo to discuss or debate so, some opt for disengagement around the topic of race altogether.

Beginning in June 2006, the combination of the survey-styled questions and the interviews was necessary because some questions were number-based or had absolute systematic answers required for the survey-styled data. Yet the interviews were aimed to tell the story of each individual principal's journey to make it to the top of the school setting, and the navigational tools he or she used as well as the pitfalls to avoid. There were key words, concepts and core belief systems that were recapitulated through the interviews. This painted a canvas of struggle, leadership styles and failures, cultural capital overtones and empowerment, race/ethnic colorblindness, gender inequality and other themes that caused dissonance and disillusionment for some interviewees.

The theoretical grounding I have acquired during my literature review work has allowed me to compare the theory with the practice of leadership and career mobility in schools through elementary school administrator's personal narrative. As Sharp and Green (1975) have noted, "[researchers] must operate simultaneously at epistemological, theoretical and empirical levels with self-awareness". Reason and Rowan (1981) advocate concepts of validity as an *interactive, dialogic logic* or *objectively subjective.* In other words, vigorously becoming self-aware and going beyond predisposition in empirical efforts establishes trustworthy data which draws on triangulation and reflexivity. When conducting the in-depth interviews, I gave the interviewees' time to reflect which in conjunction with the theoretical perspectives which assisted to integrate information into a concise qualitative comparison of the mobility process in the two countries featured.

In Ghana, the connection to the broader research of Sub-Saharan Africa and education leadership can help to inform Canadian leadership practice in terms of the strong community alliance and mobilization. In turn, Canada is strong on individual leadership models that stem from both convergent and divergent themes of competitive and cooperative practices within their leadership politics. Both fed into the strengths of one another which the results will inform both country's educators and their communities. It is also important to note that both Ghanaian and Canadian education administration history have important differences, but also some equally important parallels, not the least of which was having British and other Western influences.

Dr. Danielle Hyles-Rainford

Chapter 2

Ripples: Educators Experience Swimming Upstream

*Leaders need to be deeply reflective, actively thoughtful, and
dramatically explicit about their core values and beliefs.*

(Bolman & Deal, 1991)

Heifeitz (1994) stated "sometimes, a directive, task-oriented style
is the most effective, and at other times, a participative, relationship-
oriented style is required." Understanding the distinctions of task and
the importance of relationship building in career mobility, will assist
in the attention needed to analyze personal and structural dynamics of
organizations.

> Career mobility will be defined as the upward mobility in an occupation
> or a change, from one job function to another, for instance, a promotion
> or change from elementary school educator to administrator.

Miner & Estler (1985) redefine career mobility as "accrual mobility, a
form of internal mobility in institutions of [higher] education. [It] occurs
through evolved jobs in which the employee accrues responsibility and/
or knowledge well beyond normal growth in the job." This term, accrual
mobility is synonymous to vertical career mobility. Horizontal mobility is
referenced in my analysis, though for my purposes it is understood in the
context of vertical mobility. It is important to note that career mobility
can be halted which is lived in the form of stagnation in an occupation or
organization.

Structural theory (Bailey & Gayle, 2003) refers to analysis that
examines the significant structural dynamics in society's interactions,
institutions, and relationships. It explores the linkages and connections
that make up the fabric of an organization. Structural analysis demands
an account of phenomena based on structural relationships within groups,

between groups and among individuals. The structural paradigm includes leadership by definition of effectively mobilizing an organization's group resources. The ideas in this study challenge the concept of a rarified, immutable structure, counter-posing solutions, such as navigational tools mentioned earlier, that may lead to significant changes.

Education Systems and Trends in Occupation and Career Mobility

Career mobility exists within organizational structures, hierarchies that are socially constructed by the policies, practices, social behaviours, values and culture of a bureaucratic organization.

> Zald and Berger (1994) define a bureaucratic insurgency as "an attempt by members of an organization to implement goals, programs or policy choices that have been explicitly denied (or considered to be not acted on) by the legitimate authority of the focal organization." *What are ways marginalized educators can be empowered by bureaucratic insurgency and assert themselves in the system?*

Much sociological theorizing on trends in the system of stratification has revolved around the *liberal theory of industrialism.* In fact, in career mobility literature broadly speaking there seems to have been few attempts to propose serious alternatives since Bell and Treiman (1973) works on post-industrialism. This industrialism thesis in general provides trends on cross-national comparisons of social mobility; it provides predictions regarding the trend toward more openness in the intergenerational transmission of occupational status.

> Consistent with the human capital theory, the *industrialism thesis* assumes, in the context of a homogeneous, open and fully competitive labour market, that occupational promotion and earnings attainment are determined largely by the training, education and work experience, since these are assumed to be functional expressions of the skills and knowledge required in professional and managerial occupations. (Erikson & Goldthrope, 1992; DiPrete, 1990)

Due to the fact that unproductive principle of labour allocation, discrimination based on race, ethnicity or gender will tend in the long run to be displaced by allocation based on characteristics achieved, looking at education and experience (Bell & Treiman, 1973). Bell & Treiman (1973) hypothesizes that the higher level of industrialized a society equates larger and direct influence of educational attainment within career status. In this context he emphasized two key points. The first key point is with increase in professional specialization, technical and administrative job skills synonymously create a rise in occupational learning. This education and work co-dependency creates a competitive job market. The second point, however, acknowledges the impediments of increased occupational status or promotion that there are substantial changes in labour force structure, increased bureaucratization, and increase in the complexity of the division of labour (Bell & Treiman, 1973; Wanner, 2005).

Connecting issues of occupational status to equity, Christensen & Townsend (2004) believe occupational justice is the enablement of individual and communal occupational needs, strengths and potential when dealing with the ideas, value systems, principles and distinctions within an organization. Mediating occupational factors are the type of economy, national/international policies, cultural values and social aspects including opportunity restrictions, occupational alienation, deprivation and imbalance. Other discussions of occupational justice have incorporated occupational exploitation, occupational marginalization, and occupational segregation. (Arnold, 1982; Allen, 1987; Lawing, Moore & Groseth, 1982; Christiansen & Townsend, 2004; Bolman & Deal, 2004) Occupational injustices are socially structured and formed; and are experienced through the occupations of daily life as ongoing, unresolved stress to individuals, communities and environments.

There has been a drastic change in employment equity, due to progressive equity strategies enforced by the Toronto District School Board (TDSB). Instrumental to this change, was the Employment Equity Task Force at TDSB whose membership consisted of various employee stakeholders including Trustee's Elizabeth Hill and Stephnie Payne. It was the Employment Equity Task Force that initiated a motion to Board to both, establish the Employment Equity Office and implement a staff census to collect staff demographic information in 2004-2005. The TDSB was the first school board in Ontario to initiate race-based statistics and other significant demographic data that other boards look to, to emulate.

This momentum has continued under TDSB's current leadership of Dr. Chris Spence, Director of Education, who has been actively working to have equal representation in school leadership that reflects all school demographics in the student populous. There is historical data dating back to 1982 up to 2011, to give credence to the Toronto District School Board to highlight the level of change achieved while gathering evidence of what sustainable change must entail. Some statistical evidence for the need of school leadership representation historically, in terms of gender and visible minority distribution in Ontario are explored in the FWTAO report on gender representation in the principalship and the Toronto Board of Education now known as the TDSB in terms of visible minority principal representation. According to Lee Stewart who researched gender distribution of principalships in Canada specifically the province of Ontario through the FWTAO (Federation of Women's Teacher Association of Ontario), he reported:

> is by far the most active among provincial federations in promoting the achievement of higher levels of female participation in positions of added responsibility. Ontario school boards were also among the most active in Canada in acquiring financial support for achieving gender equity. Provincial and ministry legislation on sex equity is as strong in Ontario as anywhere, and stronger than in most jurisdictions. Yet this is not reflected in principalships in elementary schools. In fact, the percentage of women principals in Ontario elementary schools is the lowest for all jurisdictions providing data [in the early 1990s]. Ontario women do achieve a much higher representation of assistant principals, however, and at the secondary school level, representation of both women principals and assistant principals is comparatively high. (Stewart, 1990; Rees, 1990)

Carr and Klassen also give us a clear statistical picture of the under-representation of visible minorities in elementary education administration, seen in the 1982 Toronto Board of Education report underscored the stark reality for racial minorities in one of the country's most progressive school boards noted that:

> ... there were 8,404 people working for the Toronto Board, of whom 665,or about eight per cent, were non-whites. This is extremely low considering that Toronto has a population of about 25 per cent non-whites. There were three black principals, but no Asians, Southeast Asians, or Native Indians at the principal

level. Of the 36 highest positions at the Board..., there was only one black and no Asians — and incidently, just four women (cited in Lampkin, 1985). The 1987 report on *Representation of Visible/ Racial Minorities in the Toronto Board of Education Work Force* indicated that little had changed. In 1987, there were only 2 (6%) visible minority principals, 6 (11%) vice-principals and 214 (9.2%) teachers at the secondary level (Cheng, 1987).

In 1982, there is identifiable discrepancies in high numbers of visible minorities working for the Toronto Board; comparatively significant low representation in school leadership for both women and visible minorities. This was and traces remain today, a system problem rooted in the need for political action and ideological transformation within Ontario school boards. Recently, there was a Toronto District School Board (TDSB) Employment Equity Workplace Census that took place in June 2006 supported by Director Gerry Connelly. It is important to note that the percentages listed combined both secondary and elementary data; and the data could not be separated based on the survey questions. The *Comparison of Women's Representation in Job Categories: TDSB 2006* with total respondents of 608, the total number of female principals or vice principals in secondary and elementary panel is 65.8%. On the outset, this data shows high statistical significance for the system as a whole; however, we do not know the specific percentage of female elementary school principals and vice principals. The *Comparison of Representation of Visible Minorities in Job Categories: TDSB 2006* with total respondents of 924 for the Principal and Vice Principal Category, the total of visible minorities principals and vice principals in the secondary and elementary panel is 178 or 19.3% (Barbara Herring & Associates, 2007). Overall, the TDSB Employment Equity Office provided a 2006 survey which produced gender and race-based statistics coupled with the new transformational leadership of Dr. Chris Spence, showed system-wide improvements in representation for visible minorities and women. We need to recognize the incremental progress, while simultaneously, understanding the system's need for bureaucratic insurgency, systemic change that the number of available positions can equate a disproportionate higher number of visible minorities to off-set the inequities of past decades of the dominant groups.

The TDSB Employment Equity and Equity departments have provided employees education in-services on the opportunity gap for visible minorities, aboriginal peoples, women and other marginalized groups such as persons of disabilities, special needs, bisexual/gay/lesbian/

transgender/transsexual/two-spirited people to raise awareness, to become active in various hiring capacities with this *opportunity gap lens* in mind. For example, in the Spring 2010-2011 Principal/Vice Principal Promotion Round (2011), the visible minority promotions were 23 out of 93 new hires, 25% and continuing in the Fall, the visible minorities were 6 out of 16, 38%. With this consciousness, the TDSB has been able to implement incremental *sustainable change* to address the opportunity gap not only from educator to vice principal, vice principal to principal but there is also sustainable change in senior administrators representation. In light of this cross-cultural study, it is important to note that regarding the ethnic distribution of leadership opportunities in Koforidua, Ghana that I do not have definitive statistical information on this and only that the issue of career mobility discrimination based on ethnicity in Ghana is a question that needs to be fully explored and developed through regional and national statistical information.

Throughout the differential or difference theoretical approach, occupation, career and social systems theories are inherently connected. The development of the systems theory in this regard is divided into three stages: (i) the theory of closed systems; (ii) the theory of open systems; and (iii) the theory of observing or self-referential systems (Luhmann; 2006). Another development in social systems theory was system transformation which includes political system transformation, economic system transformation, cultural system transformation and normative system transformation (Zimmermann, 2004). On an international level, Wells (2005) demonstrates "that rather than a transnational convergence of policy and practice in educational institutions, what occurs – and is expected to occur when global trends are encountered in the local context in some form of hybridization."

Applying such theories of occupational/career mobility to suit the purposes of this study, we might say that where we find an 'open system' that incorporates elements of economic and cultural transformation, the goals of the systems transformation are partially met and forms of inequity would diminish. For instance, Moulton (2004) assesses in many West-African nations the benefits and shortcomings of a "top-down and system-wide reform of the education system, based on a technical, comprehensive plan for improving quality, equality and access at the primary level" or in the USAID goal for the Functional Literacy Program to carry out the eradication of illiteracy in Ghana by 2011, a cultural and normative open system change. In this broad way, we could conclude that systems transformation is the future direction of both Ghana and Canada. However, to add substance to such predictions about system change and occupational mobility specifically, it is useful to look at the specific paths, accumulated supports and barriers faced by those who were successful in upward transitions. In the case of this research, I turn attention toward elementary school education promotion in the past, looking at, among other factors, the attributes and trends of the careers and actions taken by current administrators.

Hegemonic Practices within Promotion Processes in the Education System

The research reviewed above examined the forces of political potency in the maintenance of power in hegemonic practices within the education systems in both Ghana and Canada. The reproduction of social inequalities (Bourdieu, 1973), the liberal theory of industrialism (Wanner, 2005) and the occupational justice (Christiansen & Townsend, 2004) theories all speak to asymmetrical power relations that play a role in attaining a promotion. (A)symmetrical power relations is central to the career mobility and social difference debate in terms, agenda-setting, positional, hidden, dialogue and conflict power relations. (Rao, Stuart & Kelleher, 1999) Other theorists have empowerment theories (Freire, 1971) and theories of internal power (Pinderhughes, 1989; Siu, 1979) that can be used as a compass to navigate through power webs designed to deny or limit access to occupation attainment. "Power in an organization is the capacity generated by relationships." (Rao, Stuart & Kelleher, 1999)

> In this view, power is the product, not only of institutional positions and authority, but of information, spirit and the specific patterns of relationships in which they are all embedded and through which they are all expressed.

In light of this, an effective career navigational tool would focus on building relationships and capacity of both individuals and groups to respond to changing organizational and external realities.

> Collective partnership, contribution, innovation and high levels of productivity exemplify a strong foundation to sustaining collegial and prolific relations within your work environment.

Bridging this gap between asymmetrical power relations, finding collective partnerships within a highly productive work environment is an access and empowerment tool.

My basic point here is that historical patterns of oppression and limited access to promotional opportunities can be used as a learning tool for current aspiring elementary school practitioners. Elementary education history, across many countries, including Ghana and Canada, has roots in the stratification of class, discriminatory practices and behaviours based on race, gender, nation and other. By remembering and not forgetting historical discrimination, it changes your relationship to your nation and your history, to one in which you have raised expectations that are engendered by emancipation and reconstruction forces. (Eyerman, 2001) Both past and present accounts of Ghanaian and Canadian education systems give us a context to what barriers visible minorities and women in education promotion face. In addition, these accounts inform the changes that need to take place in terms of equitable practices of educational career mobility. As part of this change potential, it is essential to know how informal networks (Heifeitz, 1994) function within schools and organizations, as well as to address individual knowledge and skill gaps by using occupational justice and empowerment practices (Christiansen & Townsend, 2004; Freire, 1971; Henry, 1998; Hall, 1996). An empowerment tool is the acknowledgement that your identity has both privilege and oppression; that you can be empowered by professionally navigating through competing societal, political, economic and cultural barriers in the elementary education system. (Arthur, Hall & Lawrence, 1989; Anyon, 1985; Arber, 1985; Acker, 1990)

By tracing the lines of sociological, transdisciplinary and traits theory, Betz; Arthur, Hall & Lawrence (1989) help us to understand the value of having *professional traits* and having "multiple positions as increasing an employee's skills and knowledge-base" for promotion. We can interpret and integrate both of these factors into education and career mobility research. In regards to educational leadership, Ronald Heifeitz (1994) has developed an experiential learning process of group dynamics and leadership which plays an integral role in understanding the systemic and social context of career mobility in education.

Career Mobility: The Importance of Leadership, Roles and Group Dynamics

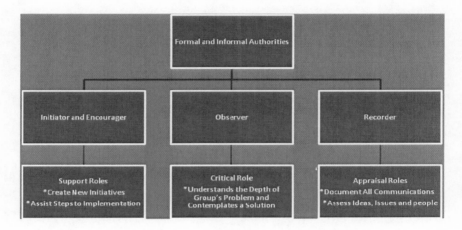

His work develops the connection between leadership, education, political science and career mobility in organizational contexts.

Career theory (Hartung, 2004) has long emphasized personal variables (e.g., abilities, needs, interests) and has only recently begun focusing on environmental variables in addressing cultural context issues. Contemporary literature on contextual variables in career attainment reflects notable movement toward recognition of the role of culture in career theory and practice. Role salience and values, which are central to developmental perspectives on careers and have been considered in other approaches, are key contextual variables that can be examined to make additional progress toward a fuller understanding of career mobility. I argue that examining the cultural dimensions of social roles and values can enrich theory and enhance practice regarding life-career development. The concepts I have introduced thus far can be integrated through a focus on three main career advancement conceptual metaphors widely recognized in the literature: the career ladder, the spiral and the web. However, it is necessary to also pay close attention to how broader forms of social difference are implicated in this type of approach.

Career Mobility

> **AN ORIENTATION TO CAREER**
> **MOBILITY AND LEADERSHIP**
>
> ### *Career Mobility*
> *** HRMO: Ladder**
> - Step-by-step progression through which an employee may advance to higher level.
>
> *** Schultz: Spiral**
> - Difference in pace and work role in terms of craft, expertise and managerial leadership.
>
> *** Holland: Web**
> - Expresses the importance of networks and affiliations between groups.
>
> ### *Education Career Mobility*
> ***Fullan, Blasé & Blasé, Lindle and Grogan & Andrews**
> - Highlight formal/informal learning and education political tactics spanning from macro to micro levels in school system.
>
> ### *Educational Leadership*
> ***Ronald Heifeitz and Marty Linsky: Exercising Leadership**
> - Confirm that leadership lies in adaptive challenges held in tension for outcome of change.

As indicated earlier, for the purpose of this study, career mobility will be defined primarily as the upward mobility of an employee in an occupation or an employee's change from one job function to another. A broader goal of this work is to understand the degree to which career mobility is an individual desire, and is determined by how savvy one is with the political, cultural and social dynamics that they confront. However, Arthur, Hall & Lawrence (1989) acknowledge the effects of *asynchronism* in dual-career family linkages, exploring the effects of traits and identities, career system strategies, implications of race and career dynamics when analyzing career advancement. The evolution of inquiry in career mobility is deeply connected to leadership.

As outlined earlier, contemporary, mainstream career theory suggests that there are three core conceptual metaphors for understanding career advancement: the ladder, the spiral, and the web. According to the Human

Resource Management Organization (HRMO, 2006), the career *ladder* consists of the grades ranging from the lowest level at which an employee can be hired as a trainee, up to the journeyperson grade level, also known as the full performance level.

> The career ladder is the *step-by-step* normal grade progression through which an employee may advance (non-) competitively to reach the full-performance level (top grade of the career ladder) of a particular job.

Career ladder promotions are neither guaranteed nor automatic, but based on individual development and performance. Managers have the flexibility to design a position structure with career ladders that can serve as a recruitment or retention tool within their organization. In school leadership context, the career ladder suggests a vertical transition to a new or advanced job function with greater qualifications implicating a skill set for the position of school administrator.

Collins (1979), Bourdieu and Passeron (1979), Bowles and Gintis (1976) all note that in order to advance through education and into the labour market successfully, one must recognize the importance of *credentialism* as it functions is status-maintaining in education employment (Collins, 1979). These authors recognize in different ways the process through which educational institutions assign occupational roles to reproduce hierarchies of social inequalities causing intergenerational transmission of socio- economic structure (Bourdieu and Passeron, 1979). How relevant is this model for an educator looking to transition from educator to school administrator? In other words, does it allow the accurate reflection of visible minorities and their reality? Burris (1983) discusses limitations of good credentials when there is an abundance of overeducated professionals which tends to produce an underemployment effect. This causes under-utilization of professional skills, and high frustration levels for those seeking promotion. It is in this context that the notion of the basic ladder model can be problematic.

The *spiral* theory considers some of the affective as well as academic combinations of successful career mobility. Schutz (2006) contributed to spiral theory by creating a four step pyramid entitled the Career Development Spectrum.

> The effectiveness of the spiral theory is the spectrum including the craftsperson, the manager, the leader, and the expert skills take time to develop, once developed the promotion happens quickly and the forward process is repeated.

The *craftsperson* stage pivots on the ability to organize skills into conscientious career planning; fueled by her work purpose to realize her ultimate contribution. The *managerial* stage represents an instrumentally driven culture focused on learning how to earn, organize and respect the financial aspect of our lives. *Personal leadership* involves a moving away from the crowd, an acknowledgment of uniqueness, a willingness to speak personal truth or speaking truth to persons in the position of power. Implicit career development at this stage involves increasing self-awareness: one must understand how aspects of one's identity differ from the status quo. The *expert* takes another kind of risk, not just differing from the status quo but challenging it based on knowledge. The expert has developed the skills, organizational abilities and courage necessary to solve problems. "Solutions are to be challenged, if they are not, they are simply recycled technique that agrees with the paradigm of the time. Essence-based work does not belong to an individual it resides in the universe; it was already there, the expert is simply a conduit." (Schultz, 2006) What makes the spiral distinct is that it incorporates many different types of roles in career development and takes into account the personal and professional needs of the employee. The Career Development Spectrum or the spiral orients to, not simply simplistic hierarchical movement up a chain of command but illuminates more nuanced differences between types of work roles one can take in the course of career mobility: craftsperson, a manager, a leader, and an expert along the way.

The career *web* is based on the work of Holland (1999) in which the *Interests* system is based. This system works on the premise that people and work environments can be loosely classified into six different groups: realistic, investigative, artistic, social, enterprising and conventional. Some people prefer certain groups because they feel more comfortable and have something in common with the people in those groups. While you may have some interests in and similarities to several of the six groups, you may be attracted primarily in two or three of the areas. The career web involves intellectual, social and emotional roles and networks centering on the process of decision-making. When doing career exploration, there are key planning assessments one needs to engage in such as self-assessment, academic/career options, occupational research, job search, decision-making, employment contacts, practical experience, career/life planning, career change (Learning For Life Resources, 2006).

> The career web is in some ways the broadest and least hierarchical orientation to career mobility, and expresses the importance of networks and affiliations between groups who have like-minded orientations to decision-making and work.

This section of the literature review on career mobility is intended to explore and define the functionalities of the three conceptual metaphors of career mobility: the ladder, the spiral and the web. Questions that emerge from these approaches that will be addressed in the analytic and synthesis chapters include the following. How will these career theories inform the research for cross-cultural and country comparison? Does Ghana or Canada seem to demonstrate an orientation to one or some over others? What is the educator's modus operandi in these terms that can explain the factors in the Ghanaian and Canadian systems? Having begun with this broad context of career mobility theory through a discussion of key conceptual metaphors, we are now in a better position to focus on education career mobility specifically.

Education Career Mobility

Garavan and Coolahan (1996) point out that there are many "barriers to career mobility that have human resource development implications." Career transition manifests itself in two main orientations: *vertical and horizontal mobility.*

> Vertical mobility refers to the movement of educators to more advanced levels, to different areas of school practice or to positions in which different functions predominate, including school administrator, autonomous professional roles (e.g. advanced practice, consultant at school board).

However, in exploring vertical mobility processes, Kanter (1977) found that those employees whose mobility was blocked, tended to exhibit matters of peer solidarity and sociability: this is what Merton (1968) terms a "horizontal orientation."

> Horizontal moves are generally perceived as less valued career paths for various reasons *generalists and specialists*, even though, it is career movement from one job function to another such as an educator to a teacher resource position, that often builds experience, expertise, understanding as well as social networks.

Educators' associations, governments and other bodies facilitate career development for teachers by means of articulated educational and career systems that provide opportunities for teachers to move from one category to another. This is horizontal mobility in practice, and educators fulfil formal (credentials), non-formal (additional qualifications or enrichment courses in classroom settings) or informal learning (all those individual and collective learning activities that we do beyond the authority or requirements of any educational institution) through this process. However, vertical mobility involves the use of social, cultural and political savvy in conjunction with formal, non-formal and informal learning activities, knowledge, skills: these are all needed for career mobility, such as from educator to school administrator (West, 1999; Bloomer & Hodkinson, 2000; Livingstone, 2004; Ryan, 2005). Therefore, a variety of factors shape career mobility, and among the other elements that this study will explore is the valuing of different factors across the elementary education systems of two different countries.

Human resources in the field of educational work address professionals as both. In the education industry, a school practitioner needs:

(1) Both a general and specialized skill-set to be successful in the promotional process. Human resources has influenced career mobility for educators by acknowledging that there has also been a major rise in the amount of knowledge and innovation pertaining to the most efficient and productive methods of streamlining workforce management policy (Human Resource Village, 2006). Writing on educational management, Fullan (2004) believes professional development must continue throughout educational careers. This includes learning that different occupational roles

form complex interrelations in educational organizations. Thus, learning related to career mobility in educational work settings needs to occur in context – not only through seminars, training courses and workshops but also through daily interactions in cultures designed for job-embedded learning and coordination.

(2) Part of this is captured in the assessments by Blasé and Blasé (1989) where they discuss personal political strategies of career mobility throughout selected work in terms of acquiescence, conformity, diplomacy, passive-aggressiveness, confrontation, ingratiation, extra involvement, visibility and advocacy are all strategies that teachers employed in their interactions with various principals in school settings. Blasé and Blasé (1989; 1991) understand that teachers exchanged tangible factors (i.e. extra work) and non-tangible factors (i.e. tactfulness, deference, humour, friendliness, support of ideas/programs, praise/recognition) for principal support (i.e. symbolic, material, technical) and, to a lesser extent, job security and advancement.

(3) Ball (1987) frequently alludes to *tactics* teachers use (for example, visibility) to further their career goals. Being *visible* allows competency to be demonstrated to larger numbers of influential members of one's organization or board. This, in turn, helps position an individual seeking promotion in an advantageous manner. However, access and equity come into question. Who is made aware of high profile assignments? Wotherspoon (2004), Fullan (2004), Blasé and Blasé (1989) and Ball (1987) all discuss a very important type of learning that is not always explicit within organizations. Political astuteness and how politics relates to career barriers and opportunities that are central to these processes and to the discussions that take place with the interviewed school principals in this study.

> The hierarchy in school boards is a pyramid with a very shallow slope (in a large board, there are dozens of teachers for every principal, dozens of principals for every superintendent, and many superintendents for one director). Those who are motivated to clamber up to the next level look assiduously for every possible advantage (Gooch, 2006).

It is a practical reality that a school leader must politically navigate as either an education administrator or a teacher attempting to move into that role. However, navigation does not simply take place within a single department or school.

> The broader *occupational-political arena of educational work* consists of five levels:
> (1) family/school relations,
> (2) micro-politics (within the school),
> (3) school-neighbourhood relations,
> (4) meso-politics (the school and the central office), and
> (5) activities at the central office of the school board itself.

Micro-politics at any individual level has been thought to be crucial. Lindle (1999) defines the term micropolitics as that which:

> represents the networks of individuals and groups within and surrounding schools; who compete for scarce resources, even power...micropolitics encompasses the daily interactions, negotiations and bargains of any school and internal and external communities. The actors in micropolitics of schools include teachers and principals, central office staff and school board members, parents and students (Lindle 1994; 1999).

Bridges (1970) has identified strategic tactics teachers typically use to influence administrators, such as bargaining, threats, bluff, flattery, exchange, exercising influence through significant others, biasing information, and dramatizing involvement. Some school leaders considered to exhibit trait pitfalls are professionally and academically known as *closed principals* (Blasé and Blasé, 1991). These are principals, according to these authors, who typically act with inequitability, unfriendliness, aggressiveness, authoritarianism, inaccessibility, nonsupportiveness, inflexibility, inconsistency, indecisiveness, ambiguous expectations, egocentricity, insecurity, and conflict avoidance. These are relevant factors for a teacher hoping to advance to consider given that career advancement in education is, in part, shaped by opportunities provided by ones principal. Blasé and Blasé (1989) further argue that:

> teachers considered the principals' ability to understand their *personal and professional needs* as crucial, and described communicative abilities in the context of their principals' willingness to engage in face-to-face interaction and deal with a range of teacher-related problems and needs...principals involved teachers broadly and directly in decision-making."

Counter-actions to navigate or contend with this type of leadership are coalition building, intermediaries, noncompliance and documentation. The political ramifications of dealing with the preliminary barriers faced when initiating one's career mobility within a *closed* leadership context could be an energy draining process, and may result in a loss of motivation to advance. Lindle (1999) states "a novice school leader learns to recognize the micropolitics of instructional leadership and advisability of respecting micropolitics."

This brings us to the broader picture in educational work life: *macropolitics*. Massaging the education system is not an easy task when dealing with increasingly strict financial accountability practices, for there can be a decreased focus on people, their skills, knowledge and abilities, in favour of results that are often financially oriented and distinct from educational practice itself. On a systemic level, macropolitics in formal education and the mobilization of human resources involve all stakeholders, staff and students alike. Fagerlind & Saha (1989) argue that productive behaviour can be partly credited to formal education especially in terms of skills and motivation levels. Thus, human capital theorists believe that an investment in education is an investment in the productivity of the population. (Downey, 1998; Lindle 1992; Ryan, 2005)

Micropolitics within individual, one-on-one interactions, *meso-politics* between the school and the board and macro-politics between all school board stakeholders in the context of, for example school board budgeting and accountability frameworks, all have a distinct dimension in this study. The interactions between human, social and cultural capital is one of the ways that this form of politics can be understood. Thus, the supports and barriers encountered in an individual educator's journey have great influence in an aspiring educators' career climb.

Quite separate from the politics of working in an educational setting, *the selection process of an influential mentor* is crucial in assisting with career navigation. Beyond formal programs of mentorship, which remain relatively rare in school boards, informal networks and social connections appear too vital for developing relationships between individuals or between groups of teachers. MacBeath (2005) argues that low tolerance of conflict is antithetical to ownership and agency when understanding first, intellectual bonding then, social bonding. West (1999) affirms informal networks and advances the discussion on formal networks by dividing it into two categories: permanent and temporary.

We can classify small groups within the school as being of one of two types, formal or informal. Formal groups are created in order to fulfill specific goals and carry on specific tasks which are clearly related to the school's overall mission. Formal groups can themselves be two types, based on the length of time over which they are convened. Permanent formal groups are bodies such as the senior management team, the various departments of the organization, staff groups fulfilling particular functions within the school organization and permanent committees. Temporary formal groups are committees or task forces which may be created to carry out a particular job but which, once the job is carried out, cease to exist unless some other task is found.

Informal networks play a large role in defining the capacity for individual agency for visible minorities and women in this study. Formal networks such as union meetings for teachers and/or subject area meetings can also play an important role for the broader development of support networks. However, important questions arise from this realization: who is included or excluded from these informal and formal networks, and do participation in such networks have equity implications for career mobility?

Grogan & Andrews (2004) advise *the use of reflective practice* and acting with consciousness when considering professional practice:

The model of reflective practitioner recognizes that novice and expert practitioners are distinguished by differences in the quantity and quality of domain-specific, declarative (know that) and procedural (know how) knowledge and associated meta-cognitive skills. It focuses attention on the need for professionals to reflect critically on situations, actions and assumptions, employing technical and practical knowledge as well as ethical criteria.

This study is in part a reflective process itself: a reflective practitioner seeking to understand the knowledge and skill gained and needed to be attained. However in investigating the topic of career mobility in education for marginalized groups including minority women, it is equally true that reflection, performance, technical and practical knowledge of the education field, and knowing what is needed to be a successful school principal is central. Formal and informal networks; and the interplay of different levels of politics within the school system are likewise important, as are an assessment of patterns of access, privilege and power. Completing the career mobility in education review, it is necessary to turn briefly to a discussion of educational leadership theory.

Educational Leadership

Ronald Heifeitz and Marty Linsky, American politics and leadership theorists, believe there are hidden values in theories of leadership.

By constantly redefining and reshaping leadership as a work in progress, Heifeitz and Linsky (2002) developed a concept in leadership entitled "the adaptive challenge". This is courageous leadership that challenges the status quo, engages value clashes for better understanding to create new paradigms for literature on leadership and systemic change.

In the article, *When Leadership Spells D A N G E R*, Heifeitz and Linsky (2006) state "leadership in education means mobilizing schools, families and communities to deal with some difficult issues – issues that people often prefer to sweep under the rug…thorny opportunities from each of us to demonstrate leadership every day in our roles as parents, teachers, administrators, or citizens in the community." Furthermore, they believe leadership often involves challenging people to live up to their words, to close the gap between their espoused values and actual behaviour. It is pointing out the unspoken issues that everyone sees and no one talks about. It often requires helping groups make difficult choices and give up something they value on behalf of something they value more. Additionally, leadership often requires finding avenues to enable people to face up to frustrating realities, such as recognizing gaps of certain groups in representative leadership, systemic barriers in promotion, budget limitations, etc.

Heifeitz points out the distinction between technical and adaptive challenges. For many challenges in the education system, experts or authorities can solve technical problems such as a computer glitch, paperwork filing problem and the like. In contrast, there are many problems that entail leadership that experts cannot technically solve called adaptive challenges. The solution lies within people. For example, organizations like school boards would prefer to treat adaptive problems as technical ones. In this line of reasoning, we could solve the problem without changing, taking a loss or giving up anything. To solve adaptive problems, we must change people's values, beliefs, habits, ways of working and way of life (Heifeitz, 1994). Arguably, human relationships are one of the most important factors in determining results in everyday professional and personal situations, and this includes those relationships found in educational work settings. Finding constructive partnerships, keeping your opposition close, acknowledging the staff and system's loss in change, accepting causalities of change and accepting responsibility for your piece of the problem are all tenets in change and adaptive leadership.

Heifeitz and Linsky's book, *Leadership on the Line* (2004) expands on their technical and adaptive work with the importance of leadership to seek sanctuary. A sanctuary provides an indispensable physical anchor and source of sustenance. It is a place of reflection and renewal, where you can listen to yourself reflecting on the sentiment of the group, where you can reaffirm your deepest sense of self and purpose. Heifeitz (1994) created the metaphors of the *leadership dance floor* (where a leader is in the thick of adaptive challenges and value clashes for change), the *balcony* (where a leader gains wider perspective of the problem to work on its solution), and the *sanctuary* (where a leader can gather his or her thoughts, capture learning lessons from painful moments and put yourself back together).

In terms of the notion of the *sanctuary,* Heifeitz and Linsky (2002) profess that how to stay alive in leadership is to have a variety of answers with none of them being easy. One answer, he believes lies in creating strategic holding environments for conflicts. He also believes that staying alive in leadership involves understanding that some solutions will stem from:

> …your ability to analyze a situation, understand the issue and what is at stake and monitor the pace of change appropriate for the people around you. Some answers emerge from your tactical ability to respond quickly to changing situations, work avoidance patterns, deviations from the plan as well as the strength of your personal life, relationships, and in your practices of renewal. (Heifeitz & Linsky, 2002)

In this study, I argue that is necessary to take their leadership thinking a step further when discussing educational promotion. Specifically, I argue that this holding environment for conflict within an organization is the tension that marginalized individuals represent within the system. This tension can raise the level of consciousness about such issues as representativeness in school leadership. This position will require adaptive work by both marginalized educators and current school leadership. The issue has been avoided in the past, but growing numbers of qualified, but persistently marginalized, professionals can, I argue, build on the tension sustain the *holding environment* to make positive change.

Career Mobility, Leadership and Emergence of Agency Attributes Data

CAREER MOBILITY

In this section on career mobility, we will examine three main aspects: (1) promotion preparation, (2) the value of horizontal and/or vertical career mobility and (3) the usefulness of career theories: the ladder, the spiral and the web. It is divided in two sub-sections to explore the differences in the Canadian respondents and then, the Ghanaian respondents. I will look at similarities in the preparation process and make suggestions of progressive difference that can inform and highlight key questions for current and future aspiring elementary school administrators to observe and implement based on the data. What is most significant about this section is first, the distinction between strategic marathon versus the ranking marathon career tactic. Second is the tangible advantage of having either horizontal / vertical mobility or not. Third is which career theory best serves aspiring school administrators in each country.

Canadian Data

Before we discuss the fluid nature of career mobility that is desired from vertical to horizontal mobility, first it is important to see how the Canadian respondents investigate the question, how does one prepare for promotion? The interviewee I want to begin with is Tony. He addresses the application preparation process for career advancement where he recommends "more in-depth interviews with other teachers, vice-principals, principals and resource teachers to get a good grasp of the people that are being promoted and seeing what is needed." Vivian's spirited suggestion in her career journey states:

> I approached my interview almost like a strategic marathon. I went to any sessions that the Board was holding on preparing for the interview; I got as much information as possible about the kinds of questions that they would ask; and the Board was very good at that time in actually having sessions of that nature, so you really needed to be prepared to speak in the interview.

Reviewing her practice, Linda suggests reviewing

> ...current board policies and practices...I also looked at our board's mission statement making sure my thought processes were in line with that as well as I went through a mock interview with several

people and they were familiar with the board interview process so that helped me get ready for the actual interview itself, reflecting on my own philosophy of education and administration.

Edmund indicates an alternative preparation method:

> I spent a fair bit of time and there was a lot of support within the board in terms of superintendents providing workshops through retired principals preparing people for the process...to get there I would like to have had different assignments-at least 2 or 3 different schools by that point so that I've had a comprehensive view of how elements are within the school board as a teacher. So basically, the plan was to move from a few schools, do different grade assignments to get my qualifications in three divisions and to find a specialist or two.

As a researcher and an educator myself, I would like to believe that the composite of these preparation tools would lead to a successful career path in school administration. Tony, Linda, Vivian and Edmund believe that mock in-depth interviews with current or retired teachers, vice-principals and principals as well as resource teachers would be a valuable asset in the preparatory stages. In addition, attending board sessions, ingraining the school board's mission statement and having a deep sense of personal awareness of one's own philosophy of education is essential. After looking at the data as a whole, I consider Vivian's attitude towards the process as accurate, viewing the preparation process as a *strategic marathon* though it is important to note that this extends beyond preparation for the interview. As we go forward with the data analysis, I argue that the *strategic marathon* initializes at conception of one's teaching career. It is important to make a conscious effort to gain valuable information from retired and current principals who have a wealth of practical knowledge and plethora of experience and expertise to share. In other words, by engaging in regular information-sharing sessions (monthly or bi-annually) with various principals you respect and can learn from would seem to be an important extension of this practice. In essence interviewees describe forms of social networking and some basic processes of building social as well as cultural capital. Such practices might support career planning in which you consciously examine and re-examine every year to hone in on the skills learned or needed, different experiences that one would need to attain in different schools, geographical locations, different grade levels and different teaching functions and leadership roles.

The next aspect of career mobility is the value given to horizontal and vertical mobility. Do both have equal value, or is one valued over the other? Jasmind believes if "you're moving horizontally from one [job] to another you're gaining experiences. They're different experiences but they're valued. They always add to the big picture." Linda supports this by adding "horizontally moving to the ministry or faculty of education or a different road" could be beneficial. Likewise, Tony feels that horizontal mobility has some merit: "some of the best experience that I received was a horizontal move from a teacher to resource position – going from working with kids to working with adults."

Paul suggests this as a new way for school boards to consider promotion and career mobility, in terms of a horizontal / vertical pendulum: an educator could move back and forth from teacher to administrator, from administrator to teacher. Paul states:

> I'd also take a look at allowing teachers to move into administrative positions and then move back to teaching – I think there really needs to be a lot more freedom of movement between the two…I think a lot of good people would go into it if they knew they could go back to teaching…good to have a broader experience of both panels, different parts of the city and work with different backgrounds.

To my mind, this is a fascinating idea that I think school boards should consider seriously. School principals are frequently the instructional leaders of their schools, the master teachers; however, there are many master teachers on any given staff. There could be limitations or resistance for excellent school administrator candidates to applying because they would miss the job function and role of teacher. This may implicate the principal associations and teacher unions negotiating. Overall, the current status of horizontal mobility amongst most of the Canadian respondents was valued in terms of specialist resource positions, working with adults, ministry positions and the like.

There are different patterns of mobility understood by the terms *ladder, spiral* and *web*. The ladder indicates a step-by-step progression; a spiral hypothesizes a variety of roles approach while a web looks at the people involved to assist one making it to their desired position. In Canada, there are many paths to school administrator. A common method is to teach for seven to ten years gaining experience in primary, junior and intermediate divisions; perhaps attain a specialist certification, gain a resource position or just be an exemplary educator and apply with the recommendation of your principal and superintendent. The incremental progression of the ladder was chosen by Giselle, Carol, Edmund and Vivian. Tony, Peter and Marina highlight their career progression as an invented *spiral-ladder*, Tony depicts it as "jumping into administration not getting lost having well-defined steps taken." Cynthia and Jasmind chose the career mobility model of the spiral; Jasmind showed "it was done in a leisurely way on my own terms based on my own pace based on my own interests. The spiral tends to give you a chance to enjoy what you're doing at a certain time." Dwayne, Oliver, Paul, Shannon and Linda chose the web. Dwayne viewed it as "the interconnectedness and different people who've helped me to get here and stay in touch with at all levels, it is important that they're moving along with me." Again, across them all while human capital and credentials matter, it would appear that practices related to social networking and social capital, and hidden beneath these process, cultural capital accumulation, are important for understanding what is going on.

Each career theory has merit and each person resonated with their personal pathways and progression. Planning and people seem to be central to all career themes. The creation of *spiral-ladder* suggests a combined orientation, and this suggests that there needs to be attention to all three career theories if we're to express all of the inter-workings of relationships, strategic step accomplishments, multiple roles, and direction. They seem to all lend itself to one another. Perhaps, using the theories as not a fixed lock-step formula but rather as a *tool kit* describes how one's career may require different items at different times and stages.

Ghanaian Data

Understanding that there is horizontal and vertical mobility, it seems prudent to explore both and see if one is valued more than the other, not simply at different phases in one's career, but in different contexts as well. In Ghana, Ado states clearly, "horizontal mobility is not valued. If you want to move up through the ranks, if a person decides not to move up the ranks, it means that he's not going to work hard." What is valued, Kwame thinks is that "you have to have experience yourself as a way of doing and also when officers coming from the Ministry office to actually attest to whether you actually live up to their expectations, then you can move forward." For moving forward in one's career, Asenso argues that you must "study the work that was given to you, the functions, the rules, the responsibilities and these are preparations to move." Selwin adds that for interview preparation the "extra courses mounted by the education department" are key to mobility success.

What we see here is that in the examples from Ghana the system is oriented much more strongly to vertical mobility, established through its specific thirteen level ranking system' for educational professionals outlined earlier in the study. In terms of vertical career mobility, Angelina and Emmanuel agree that there is competition for scarce resources in terms of school administration jobs in Ghana; Rose thinks it is more common that most people "remain in their jobs until the head retires…and that could be five to ten years or more." Angelina argues that "there needs to be more vacancies." In this sense, her point recognizes a structural disconnect between the ranking system and the number of positions available for a capable workforce in school leadership. The Ghanaian education system is structured for continual strides for educational attainment and lifelong learning of skills but many educator professionals seem to plateau and are in this holding environment waiting and waiting for their break or opportunity to come and it may only be when "there are more vacancies and openings to as many people from different backgrounds and schools… they only want to promote somebody in their same school to replace the one who is either leaving, transferring or going on retirement…only in rural areas, in remote parts of the country have young [principals] heads but in bigger towns, NO [opportunity]!", Emmanuel says.

This situation creates a climate of intense competition and fear for current administrators like Angelina, who worries you must "work harder otherwise you may be demoted or lose your position." There seems to be a fear of serious consequences if the traditional pattern of the ranking system is not followed or work performance *checks-and-balance* are not met. As recently established in Ontario, there is also no union for principals in Ghana but there is a network association to share ideas for success and to provide learning opportunities. Many educators who are frustrated and are tired of waiting take this route that Jennifer describes. She indicates "it is easier to get promoted in rural areas because the government has given some incentive to teachers who go to remote areas. They have to sacrifice for their promotion."

Deeply shaped by Ghana's education profession ranking system, thirteen out of fifteen respondents said the *ladder* describes their promotion process. There are thirteen steps to promotion from Certificate "A" to Director General. The order is as follows: (1) Certificate "A", (2) Superintendent II, (3) Superintendent I, (4) Senior Superintendent II,

(5) Senior Superintendent I, (6) Principal Superintendent, (7) Assistant Director II, (8) Assistant Director I, (9) Deputy Director, (10) Director II, (11) Director I, (12) Deputy Director General and (13) Director General. The hierarchy of the education system appears based on objective forms of progression but which can also be more rigid than those seen in the Toronto, Ontario context. It is important to look at the description of the roles to gain a better understanding of the Ghanaian education professional ranking system or the placement of teaching staff model.

However, this is not to say that other patterns of progression are completely excluded. Emmanuel believes "that when you follow the ladder principle, you attain the highest qualification and then as you work you acquire the skills and you are able to manage the school better." In other words, for some the ladder may be used to describe how one attains a position, but the ability to work effectively in that position requires additional development that may, in some cases, depend on other forms of capital accumulation. Nii and Bettina go a step further. They speak of an interesting combination of a *web-ladder* to describe their career progression. Nii acknowledges initializing the process reaching the first step on the ladder or the ranking system "a lot of people give information and their experience, I would take the web before you can get to the ladder." Likewise, Bettina sees merit in the web and ladder like Nii, she says "it's entangled, everybody takes part in the web for you to do the work- so you use the web to move around then, the ladder comes in to help you move and climb." Selwin, however, raises an important point. He does not think the web is a good idea "because you can get locked...or your hands get tied, you can't move forward."

There is much to be learned from the highly structural Ghanaian ranking system of career discipline and performance stamina each educator and principal must maintain throughout their career. Unlike Canada, horizontal mobility appears less valued due to organizational structure and tight guideline restraints. However, people and planning are also constant themes for Ghanaian respondents. The ranking system expresses the importance of forms of human capital accumulation. However, the creation of the *web-ladder* also implies the limits of career theories and the need for overlapping or multi-purpose methods for effective career analysis and practice. Upon closer inspection of the data, the community in the *web-ladder* for the initial stages of entry in the education system is just as important as their involvement in the interview processes for each step on the ranking system. Making sacrifice for rural areas or waiting for vacancies for years are what aspiring Ghanaian educators tend to face. While issues of supply and demand, and too many qualified teachers for limited principal positions are at play here, having forms of community support and an attitude of sacrifice and determination are key to career mobility in Ghana.

LEADERSHIP

In this section on leadership, we will examine three main aspects: (1) about exercising leadership and what is meant by hard work, (2) the value of community, respect and integrity at work, and (3) the value of both good and poor examples of leadership. It is divided in two sub-sections to explore the Canadian respondents and then, the Ghanaian respondents. Below I look at the distinctions in school leadership practices such as sustainable or transformation leadership in Canada, and the discourse of the 'work hard' ethic in Ghana. Other highlights are discerning the current needs of the various school boards involved on a systemic and school leadership level as well as exploring the expectations of leadership in the school, school board and wider-community expects of school leaders in each country.

Canadian Data

Amongst the Canadian respondents, there were various terms associated with leadership such as sustainable, transformational, professional learning communities and leadership by demonstration. Vivian recognizes that "in a school culture that empowers people to take on different roles that provides invitations for people for leadership, I think that enhances someone's likelihood of being recognized and promoted. It gives them a good training ground for…sustainable leadership." This ignites the question, where do we learn how to exercise leadership, as well as who exactly is invited to participate in this culture and these networks of learning? At the same time, Giselle believes that we learn just as much or more from poor examples of leadership than good ones, perhaps learning what not to do. She claimed "I learned a lot from poor examples – [where] I felt principals were poor examples [they] were more managers than people…leadership where people respect one another, is the most important [thing] in this job…the more that you are known in the school board, the better chances there are for advancement." Edmund believes "you need to demonstrate leadership within the school…show comprehensive view of the school in terms of how to handle situations and how to further student progress…show some leadership… engage [in partnerships] in a variety of community situations." Shannon expands on that idea by taking a systemic approach, "our whole board is built on the image of professional learning communities…built on the concept of transformational leadership."

From the observations on individuals in leadership roles, and his/her (learned) traits as well as seeing them using sustainable and transformational leadership. Through effective outreach of school-community partnerships and participating in school board initiatives and professional teams, I came to see that there is more to exercising leadership than is often thought. I will extend this reasoning to a belief that we can learn about leadership in every moment that we are interacting within an organization or school setting, whether it is through observing or experiencing leadership failures or successes.

Ghanaian Data

In light of the ranking system set up by the Ghanaian Ministry of Education, there is a pre-set career mobility path. It appears to be a path that majority of educators understand, respect and *work hard* to abide by. Interestingly enough, all fifteen Ghanaian interviewees oriented consistently to the notion of *work hard* and yet only occasionally mentioned by the Canadian interviewees. It begged the question, what meaning did the respondents assign to this standardized phrase, and what implications did it have for practice? This notion of *work hard* was elaborated on concisely, for example, by Elaine who stated "work stamina, learn hard and be useful to the community." Likewise, Yvonne explained that working hard related to "dedicating yourself, always learning, take part in community" and Kwame described it as "gallop[ing] through ranks with merit and handl[ing] school affairs with unity in relationships." Bettina emphasized that "your knowledge and your intelligence about the particular work of education and having the ability to distinguish yourself from another person. Take courses and help yourself improve." The convergence of their conversations around the *work hard* notion expresses determination in professional life, conflict and change in the affairs of the school, and links academic excellence with an understanding of the importance of both collegiality and community collaboration.

If there was a wish list, Selwin "would like to tell higher education authorities to give a *free hand* to principals so that they can put elements they need into their school to enable the children to be trained so that one day they will be good citizens to live in the country." Asenso echoes the need for decentralized control and more power and freedom should be given to the principal by stating "the principal is the school leader, you should be able to set up your own programs and implement them". What seems clear is that in Ghana, the education system has a strong structure oriented to step-by-step procedures for almost every facet of education; not simply for career advancement but for the operation of schools themselves.

Nala believes "if you respect yourself and respect others, others will respect you as a leader. If you say you are going to do something, do it in the timeframe you have." Nala points out the importance of respect and integrity in a school leader but Yvonne looks not only at virtue but lived, daily practice. Yvonne understands how important it is to have "good examples of leadership" for aspiring teachers and current administrators. Ado supports this idea with a similar philosophy to lead by example, "I try to live an exemplary life" and Jennifer by "setting a good example" for our successors. Ado calls each one of us to task to be the change we want to see in the world by living an exemplary life, be the example that you would like to see as a teacher as well as when you make it as a school administrator.

AGENCY ATTRIBUTES

In this section, there are ten "agency attributes" that I wish to explore. We will examine two main aspects, the qualitative and quantifiable attributes. Many of the attributes can have a mixture of both qualitative and quantitative. For the purposes of this study, I divided the ten career agency attributes into the two main aspects. First, the qualitative attributes that surfaced in the Canadian interviews were *international experience, seniority, influential mentorship, high visibility assignments, political astuteness, innovation and creativity added to your organization and personal style.* Second, the quantifiable attributes that materialized were *superior job performance, higher education and a good relationship with management.* We will see that some attributes overlap (e.g. *seniority and political astuteness*). It is divided in two sub-sections to explore the differences in the Canadian respondents and then, the Ghanaian respondents.

The combination of the qualitative and quantifiable agency attributes help us to see that written appraisals, teaching documentation, credentials and qualifications are highly valued among education professionals in Koforidua, Ghana. In Ontario, personal style, creativity, relationship building, dynamics and politics play a comparatively larger role in the context of everyday living and working environments within our education system. In both societies, higher education takes on a key role. However, access to *higher education* is the mitigating factor: a huge obstacle for many Ghanaians. Both systems have performance appraisals but this did not appear to be as important in Canadian interviews compared to those from Ghana. In part, this could be due to the fact that there is an evaluation process for each rank or thirteen steps in the Ghanaian promotion grid. There are structural, systemic and cultural differences that present themselves as we go through this section.

Canadian Data

The breadth and depth of an educator's experience is difficult to standardize. It takes on many hues and tones over the years. The spectrum ranges in various geographical locations, grades and divisions, specialist positions or overseas opportunities. Oliver, a respondent with a plethora of *international experience,* feels "in order to become an educator in an administrative facet – many avenues have to affect your education and your own personal growth. I myself have taught in many different countries, come back to Canada with that information and it helped me grow as an educator and also as an administrator." Like Oliver, I believe international teaching or educational opportunities have learning contours that can be different than, the Western context of our education system. The breadth of diverse educational experience can provide moments of mastery in teaching and challenge the deepest competence levels of one's professionalism while enduring a rigourous learning curve within international contexts. And yet, the depth of an international experience can open up your mind and heart to education and children providing a renewal of purpose and vocation.

Teaching and administration is a vocation. The years accumulated over the span of one's career are the basis of your *seniority:* a matter that is much more than simply the number of years one has been in an occupation. However, it is important to ask: what kind of experience is valued of an educator on his/her journey to educational leadership? Shannon explains:

> Seniority is valuable if each year you are in a school you gain new experiences. If you've been teaching thirty two years in Grade 2 and that's all you do, you have lots of seniority but it's not the valuable kind that you need in order to bring a wealth of experience as an administrator. You have to change grade levels – you have to change

schools and you have to have a wide variety extracurricularly to take a serious intention to become an administrator.

The breadth and depth of varied national and international educational experience, or even business or community work appears to be valued to a degree in the Canadian data. But, it raises the question of how an aspiring educator knows what grades to teach, what areas to be trained in, or what country to go to? For any of the above questions and more, an *influential mentor* or coach is monumental in the process of navigation toward the goal of becoming a school principal. Marina was fortunate enough to have one right at her school:

> The supervisor that I had at that time was very good. She was actually my principal at the time and she got a group of aspiring leaders together and went through interviews with us, mock interviews. She critiqued the interviews and talked to us about it…now, I mentor a lot of younger principals but I'm very approachable, I'm very down to earth, I'm very grounded. I can talk to them about what it's like to be a brand new principal and try to understand the experiences they're having and try to give them what I have gained over the years as a principal.

Finding such mentors is a difficult challenge. They are an essential but often hidden resource for aspiring teachers. In addition, where the process of engaging a mentor is informal and strictly self-guided, a variety of potential inequities may emerge. Who finds it most easy to develop these types of relationships with whom? Social networking, shaped by hidden forms of cultural knowledge privileged within a school, in part, predict a process of social reproduction in gender and racial terms specifically.

Gaining access to *high visibility assignments* may be an important means of raising one's profile in a school, but it is not an easy thing to accomplish. Vivian describes the basic process when she states "I think to be able to get into some kind of a higher profile position where you're working as a member of a committee at the board level – you need to 'up' your profile so that people see you." The *political astuteness* or savvy it requires is to first gain credibility on the school board level. Beyond having the right credentials, an educator would have to start out with assisting other school board personnel's vision and projects and see it flourish to its success. This invites teachers to be *team players,* which includes certain dangers of reproducing forms of hierarchy, but in any case it requires careful observation of political dynamics, inter-relations amongst people and social networks. Trying to gain exposure to different situations and people, this is a political matter. This basic dynamic is at play even once one becomes a principal. Edmund discusses this aspect of schools and school boards in this way:

> Well everything's political to some degree. I think that as principal within the organization you're basically a middle manager. You do need to follow what the board is telling you to do, and then you're the medium between staff and the board, so you are the agent of the board but the board is this amorphous organization that is outside of the building so sometimes you need to deflect elements that the board is asking you to do because you need to protect your school and your staff. At the same time if you're getting a lot of push back you need to figure out a way to bridge, broker and modify what you're being asked to do and again this is a key piece, how supportive is your superintendent? I've always had very supportive superintendents and if they're supporting you to have a little latitude. The principal's job can be one of the most creative you can have and that is rewarding.

Being able to sustain the support can be translated into doing the elements that can help the people that can help you. Paul feels in terms of promotion, the hiring committee "also looks for some kind of *innovation*, some kind of *creativity*." According to the interview data, having initiative is good and can add value to your school board to some extent, however, you cannot pose a threat by your ideas; you can't show people up. It is important to get to know your superiors, principals, superintendents on a personal level. This obviously entails some significant social networking, the building of social capital. It also suggests the possibility that important errors in belief, and in some cases inequities, can be difficult to address. Paul takes this point further when he expresses that *personal style* is important, the "ability to be persistent, it proves that people who were promoted had a certain doggedness to them that kept them going…for my interview I just tried to present myself- warts and all and listen with some care to the questions I would be answering." Here we might ask ourselves the degree to which *personal style* is what fits the race and gender as well as class-based norms of the school system. And in this regard specifically, Linda goes on to say she believes "promotion is based on personality not race." We can ask, however, how exactly can these elements be separated? Separating one's social 'role' from one's broader social being or 'self', for example as a minority woman, can be complicated (e.g. Heifeitz 1994), if not impossible. And, the call for such separation calls into question the instances where the privileged social group in a board or any other workplace is not asked to do the same thing.

Ghanaian Data

Seniority plays a large role in the Ghanaian education system. Bettina uses an "educational management tool that states particulars of teacher's charts and so it includes the years of service, the ranks in years from 1-39 years." Kwame and Grace both discuss historical trends in seniority and promotion. Grace states "in colonial days, you have to teach for 10 years before you climb one step but these days three years you have to teach then you interview for the next step on the ranking system." Emmanuel offers another view of historical comparisons:

> you could spend more than 15 to 20 years in the classroom before you were appointed in the past. Presently, if you are lucky to work for five years and you are able to attain your first degree, you are potential to be head of an elementary institution. They now combined academic work and experience to be appointed to head not just experience alone.

Emmanuel continues and gives some insight into the seniority debate, he states "seniority plays a greater role if a junior is head; those who are senior to him will have very little respect for him in some cases. If the person is senior to them, they grumble within them but it doesn't come into the open and they are bound to obey the one in authority." On the other hand, Nii and Ado are current principals who moved through the ranking system at a younger age than many in the Ghanaian education system advancement paradigm, they assert competence and teamwork or social savvy will combat such discrepancies. Nii rebuts for our purposes and states "competence is key not year range and seniority, whether you are 30 or 40 years of age, you are given the position of principals because of your competence." Ado expands this a bit further however saying, "as I'm 36, I am the head and I'm the youngest person among this staff but they afford me that respect because I don't impose elements on them. We come together." Ado seems to understand the social and political savvy it takes to not only stay afloat but direct the "school leadership" boat with all staff sailors on board. Likewise, Emmanuel states "if there are more people who are more competent than you and you happen to be their head, they will see the lapses in your administration and they will erode your authority base. They need to see you have a lot of wisdom, bring out your experience, win their respect and they will support your administration."

It is a tall task but this is where *political astuteness* comes in: an expression of the strategic use of multiple forms of capital accumulated in the past and exercised in the form of competence in the present and future. Nii, Ado and Emmanuel recognize the winning combination of competence and knowledge; it should not be read as these respondents are not simply trying to assimilate to fit in to the dominant group, they can and do assert issues of inequity and agency.

Selwin's learning curve was steep for his crash course in political astuteness, Selwin was

> ...appointed to the school but people who were already in the school wanted somebody who was on the staff to be appointed. I was appointed from somewhere else to join so they came together against me...I tried to bring them over on my side. You let them know the essence of the work they are doing and they begin to do it.

Asenso says "personally let me say this, political networks have worked against me." Ado's explanation may assist to shed light into why. He says "others will draw you out of your line so that you could be derailed; you go off your professional course." The lack of support and intentional professional derailment could be caused by personal gripes and misunderstandings or unsuccessful collaborative professional practices within the school or school board networks. Yvonne, however, sees these forms of conflict as constructive: "sometimes you have to have clashes in your values for your constituents, your organization to grow." Kwame views politics as part of human nature. He says "human nature as it is; is that at times in some organizations if somebody comes from your area, ethnicity or neighbourhood, you support them or encourage the education authorities to give them the job." Ado agrees with this response, his comment is "to be very honest the hiring is not what it should be whereby there are competitions where there are others who sometimes tend to be biased, in favor of people from their family line." With this we begin to get a sense that the objective career ladder of the Ghanaian system includes even more complications.

Part of responding effectively to such complications requires understanding complex forms of favouritism that can lead to inequity and upset an otherwise objective and fair system of career progression. Class privileges also come into play. Kwame states in Ghana "the rich people buy their way through because they have better aggregate for the school." Jennifer shares a story, "I knew a new principal's father bought a house for the teachers…he used his influence". The financial implications of those who are well-off in Ghana, include buying favour for career mobility is an important matter to be addressed. The economic hardships of the school system make it more vulnerable in this regard.

Despite inequities, respondents often argued that personal traits of, as Grace put it, "integrity, educational background and work stamina" are what define successful career advancement. Nala underlines this when she describes accountability practices: the school board is watching,

> …you're work performance; they study me…all that I am doing. They are checking your punctuality, your reliability, the way you work out elements, the way you move with your teachers - how you talk to them, how fair and firm, how you handle everything in the school especially the children.

Likewise, Asenso believes "the distinguishing factor from the candidates is their performance. The experience they have acquired in their service, that all children under you pass through the school and succeed …and in Ghana here, must attain the highest level of academic performance." According to Ado, superior or excellent performance on the job entails "excellence because there are other places that are looked at, like initiative and then sometimes it could be classroom work. This is shown on their appraisal." Mensa thinks it is important to make a conscious decision and discern whether you are a generalist within education or a specialist. He feels "it is important to have a specialist. I upgraded my academic standards and I am now a specialist in home economics." He believes that having a specialist in education many give you an advantage. Carving out a niche with your field and be recognize for a particular competence or skill may help to prove your usefulness to your organization.

Another useful and essential navigational tool is building and *maintaining a good relationship with management.* Emmanuel supports this by revealing "it's very, very important that people learn to understudy other people and pick the good aspects of administration to groom them to become good leaders in the future." Asenso indicates that he

> …looks out for teachers who are due for promotion, I call them into my office and start my own in-service training for them. I tell them what they have to look out for when they attend an interview…it is the responsibility of the principal. It is my place to help them. When they're vacancies in other schools, I look around my faculty and know there's somebody who can do it. I encourage them to apply.

The last of the three qualitative agency attributes is *higher education*. Asenso asserts "the factor here is that you need to attain a university degree and down here it is very difficult, getting down to the university is very difficult and very costly. Very costly for us…higher than some people can attain…now, you must be a university graduate to be the rank of principal." In this case, the marginalized groups is the rural to suburban high school graduates that do not have the financial means to attend university and achieve the bachelor's degree which is required in most cases to become a teacher in Koforidua, Ghana. Proximal distance, cost of transportation, books, degree program, or even social assistance in many cases are just not a tangible reality exclaims Asenso. The cost, not the desire or intellectual ability, is the barrier to professional advancement in the education field. I wonder how many self-educated teacher professionals are in the midst of the community, empowering children informally. These people should be able to teach formally, however, education policies and financial restraint keeps these talented, insightful individuals out of the classroom and essentially, out of the education career track altogether.

That the respondents orient to elements within rather than beyond their control in their attempts to progress toward educational leadership should not be a surprise. Here we have seen a range of strategies, practices and knowledge-building that individuals can use to progress in their careers. I have also begun to introduce that there are systems of favouritism and privilege that shape the process as well. Thus, we can ask further questions. Who is it that receives the rewards of such efforts, knowledge-building and strategizing? Is it even across all aspiring teachers or do certain privileged groups appear to have advantages?

Chapter 3

Waves: Educators Embody Swimming Upstream

Power is an often unspoken but central dynamic in cross-cultural encounters.
We have observed its presence in the associations of dominance, superiority,
and denigration, with ethnic identity, and group status; in the common
perception of difference from others as "better than" or "less than"; and
in the dynamics of race (racism), which is itself a power system.
(Pinderhughes, 1989)

INTERROGATING CAREER MOBILITY AND LEADERSHIP IN TERMS OF POWER AND SOCIAL DIFFERENCE

Race, Power and Leadership: West, James, Dei and Pinderhughes
*look at limitations the system places on certain racial and ethnic groups in terms of their ability to move up and how race informs decisions about promotion.

Understanding Everyday Racism: Philomena Essed
*understands racism as complex system of power, shapes social relations and practices.

Gender, Power and Leadership: Smith, Kimmel, Wane, Hill-Collins and Hooks
*assert gender inequity in leadership is rooted in biased institutional power arrangements including female glass ceiling, male escalator effect, and cultural distinctions in feminisms.

The Emancipation of Women-An African Perspective: Florence Abena Dolphyne
*distinguishes women from feminism due to cultural contexts specific to Africa.

> ### *Gender Leadership-Western Context: Aruna, Rao, Stuart and Kelleher*
> *Gender power relations in terms of position, agenda, hidden, dialogue and conflict.

Race, Power and Leadership

A variety of researchers have analyzed factors that shape issues of race and power. Fanon (1963), Freire (1971), West (1993), Pinderhughes (1989), Troyna (1994), James (1996), Arber (2000), Lopez (2003), Delgado (2003) and Dei (2005) look at the limitations the system places on certain racial and ethnic groups in terms of their ability to move in an advantageous direction and, by implication, how race informs decisions about promotion. Cornell West (1994) argues that progressive leadership deserves cultivation and support. This new leadership must be grounded in grassroots organizing that highlights democratic accountability. Within educational work settings, support around race and how it informs present and prospective leadership are positively affected by community efforts to create change through the acknowledgment of racism. Similarly Siu (1979) suggests "power is the universal solvent of human relations." The power relationships between people determine whether their interactions are characterized by dominance-subordination or equality.

> Empowerment requires the use of strategies that enable people to experience themselves as competent, valuable, and worthwhile both as individuals and as members of their cultural group (Freire, 1971).

Power motivates many of our societal values: status, perfection, possession, achievement, competition, independence, etc. Powerlessness is indicative of a painful social situation often devoid of these qualities. In discussing the effectiveness of her treatment model, *ethnotherapy*, Klein weighs the consequences of what she calls *double-victimization* (Klein, 1980). Klein echoes W.E.B. Dubois notion of *double consciousness*. (Dubois, 1903) The sense of entitlement which power can create prepares an individual to cope with adversity or situations in which she lacks power. Powerlessness also has relevance for cross-cultural interaction and work. Powerlessness is painful; people tend to respond in ways that will neutralize their pain with strategies that enable them to turn that powerlessness into a sense of power. One response that is commonly cited as a strategy for turning powerlessness into power is that of personal mastery and achievement (Pinderhughes, 1989).

Beverly Jones in Carl James' article (1996) understands the notion of:

> *a dominant culture, that every society has one.* Institutions are formed around the assumptions of this dominant culture.

Yet because the dominant culture doesn't have to look outside itself, it remains chiefly unconscious of its own characteristics and assumptions. Carl James (1996) understands "within all cultures exist subcultures." A subculture may be defined as a group of people within a larger sociopolitical structure who share cultural (and linguistic) characteristics, which are distinctive enough to distinguish them from others within the same culture (Hoopes and Pusch, 1981).

> Understanding subordination, oppression and race has importance within this study. My point here is that powerlessness and empowerment is implicated in the relationship between *dominant cultures* and the sub-cultures which exist within it. These interrelations represent what is called cultural capital which plays an important role in shaping agency in career mobility for marginalized professionals including visible minorities and women. Power is not neutral; the cultures that have power sustain it.

When we live in a time where we are all on an equal playing field, where there is only one game with equal power, access and opportunity, there would be no need to make distinctions between dominant and minority groups but until then and for the purposes of this study, I will use dominant and minority group. Sub-cultures or minority groups are faced with multiple choices revolving around the strategic development of dominant cultural capital and/or develop and accumulate their own collective sub-cultural capital and power, in the course of which the possibility for system change may emerge.

The suggestion of personal agency and mastery to combat the painful predicaments and anguish of this is central to confronting barriers in the system. If one experiences oneself as competent, confident and valuable then, the organization will not interpret this member of a subculture pejoratively as suffering from some kind of *victim syndrome,* rather, this person can begin to operate out of internalized power. The possibility of contribution in this space of *internalized power* is endless in terms of race and professional growth, because the barriers are now externalized. The amount of pain experienced by being shut out of the larger culture due to race or other barriers, turned around into internalized power, could significantly enlarge the depth of contribution to one's organization and change in one's own community. Anti-racism education presents one strategy that works to achieve this precise effect. Dei defines anti-racism education as an action-oriented strategy for institutionalized, systemic change, working to address racism and the interlocking systems of social oppression (Dei, 1996).

In terms of this anti-racist education, how are we to conceptualize this *internalized empowerment* Klein writes about, in the face of dominance or powerlessness? How are we to understand the relations between this internal empowerment and the operations of race and racism? We can begin to think about race and racism in terms of two categories: as an ideological phenomenon, and as a specific set of social practices, actions or activities. From this we can then begin to think about strategies for dealing with minoritization in terms of career mobility. Smith (1999) states that:

> To acquiesce is to lose ourselves entirely and implicitly agree with all that has been said about us. To resist is to retrench in the margins, retrieve what we were and remake ourselves. The past, our stories local and global, the present, our communities, cultures, languages and social practices all may be spaces of marginalization, but they may have also become spaces of resistance and hope. (Smith cited in Dei, 2005)

In fact, racism dominates our society even though it might seem very subtle at times (Castanga & Dei, 2000). *Critical anti-colonial thought* furthers an understanding the issues of culture, race, identity, and representation. Here the 'colonial' dynamic is conceptualized as an "imposed and dominating" presence, like a *shark phenomenon* (Dei & Asgharzadeh, 2001). The anti-colonial framework seeks to dissect how colonialism is reproduced and affects the power relations within an institution and in professional development. This perspective highlights the implications of imperialism on knowledge production, agency and subjective politics (Dei & Asgharzadeh, 2001; Delgado 2003; Fanon 1963; Foucault, 1980).

Internalized racism must be brought to light to prepare oneself to be effective in building a collective structure for resistance that does not reproduce processes of racism amongst its own members. That is why anti-racism work, and work to expose all other forms of oppression, is imperative. Bivens (1995) defines internalized racism as

> ...the situation that occurs in a racist system when a group oppressed by racism supports the supremacy and dominance of the dominating group by maintaining or participating in the set of attitudes, behaviours, social structures and ideologies that under-gird the dominating group's power.

Ryan (2003) sees the issue through a similar lens; he argues that a liberal interpretation of internalized racism does not do justice to the intersectional complexity of the race, gender and class which functions within the family, the school and the world.

> This relates to this study by showing the effects of asynchronic power to the dominant group and how that sustains power in the education promotional process and the implications of access to school leadership positions for marginalized groups.

On the other hand, it adds a layer of complexity to the study by acknowledging internalized racism amongst unsupportive members of visible minority groups that may work to sustain systems of privilege. The next layer of the study manifests in these questions: are their possibilities for dominant and visible minority groups to be supportive allies? Do women in the dominant group support female visible minorities? How can cross-cultural groups form discussion groups or engage in conversations to address these issues? What supporters and dissenters are there and what are their effects? Is there such a concept of race neutrality, pluralism or racism -- if so, how do these concepts actualize and manifest themselves within organizations? In the next section, I draw on the work of Philomena Essed to shed some light on this as she takes us through observations in her study of understanding everyday racism.

Understanding Everyday Racism

Philomena Essed (1991), African-American and Dutch sociologist, contends that everyday racism is based on the understanding of general features, experience and the way processes of racism restrict the goals and opportunities of one's group.

> Essed (1991) defines "racism as power in terms of cognitions, actions, and procedures that contribute to the development and perpetuation of a system in which dominant culture manage" visible minorities.

On the other hand, it adds a layer of complexity to the study by acknowledging internalized racism amongst unsupportive members of visible minority groups that may Note that racial domination, as I pointed out earlier, interacts with dynamic forces of gender and class. She sees the need for an alternative approach, supporting the experienced reality. "To conceptualize how racism, as a complex system of power, shapes the ways in which social relations and practices are actually experienced by [visible minority] women, I draw on major insights of some people who have worked on the notion of power" (Essed, 1991). To define her concept of power, Essed integrates macro and micro dimensions of racism which she adopted from Arendt. As Essed explains, Arendt (1970) argues that power is never the property of an individual but it belongs to a group as long as the group stays together. Therefore, *power pertains to the human ability not only to act but to act in concert.* Arendt's view of power provides a basis for understanding the crucial role of racist ideologies, not only as rationalization of existing inequalities but also as determinants of future uniformity of action.

In order to analyze accounts of racism, Essed made a table of reconstruction categories and *heuristics* of accounts in these five categories: context, complication, evaluation, argumentation and decision.

> The forms of heuristics are comparison, inference, comparison for consistency, comparison for consensus and comparison for inconsistency.

She applied the reconstruction categories to case scenerios of her respondents. One part of Essed's (1982 cited in Essed, 1991) study was looking at the racist complications in job applications. The question, have you ever experienced discrimination when you applied for a job? Was met with various answers, some focusing on the structural exclusion of [visible minority] women from leading positions, others on the creation of ethnic sectors of work and the marginalization of that type of work

> …actions do not only consist of elements people do, verbally or non-verbally, but also of elements people do not do. Not doing something one would normally expect in a situation is an important mechanism of racism, called *passive racism.*" Essed related two case scenarios around job applications.

To explain her analysis I would like to focus on her respondent, Micky.

> Micky T. applied for a job at the campus accounting office. The personnel manager said she was very busy and asked her to return on Monday, which was fine with Micky T. On Monday, Micky T. called first to see whether the lady she wanted to see was in. Her secretary answered the phone and said she had gone on vacation. And the job had been filled. (Essed, 1991)

Essed indicated in her accounts that Micky had an accent; language, race and cultural issues go hand and hand. By the employee of the company giving her misinformation, inferred accent bias and diverting job process for a later time all are incongruent with a standard job application process.

This case reflects everyday racism in obtaining jobs but even after you do initialize into an organization there is still other "hoops" and barriers of race and social difference that one has to navigate. Essed's development of racism and job application discrimination can be compared to the data analysis in this study to see if there are significant indicators of change from then to now.

As has been seen, each section of this literature review is meant to add a piece to the puzzle to develop a cumulative picture of career mobility in general and in relation to educational work specifically. I continue to develop this cumulative picture with a discussion of gender and power by drawing on the work of, first, some Western theorists and then later on the Ghanaian gender theorist, Florence Abena Dolphyne.

Gender, Power and Leadership

A method of thinking about gender, power and leadership is feminist epistemology. It starts from women's actual lived experiences, a method that encompasses the variations in their experiences. (Dorothy Smith,

1990) Experience, for this study, will be central to the analysis. However, in addition according to Hoshchild and Politt (Cited in Kimmel, 2000) in the historical development of gender discrimination, there were three gender ideologies in the workplace to register that shape experience: *homosocial reproduction* (work reinforces a man's pride, self-respect, status and manhood), *emotional work* (enhancing male consumer experience i.e. stewardess), and *job segregation* by gender.

> Kimmel (2000) described the twin barriers women face in two analogies building on the original notions of *the glass ceiling* and *the sticky floor* which combine to keep women stuck at the bottom and unable to reach the top. The sticky floor keeps women trapped in low wage positions, with little opportunity for upward mobility. The glass ceiling consists of artificial barriers, based on attitudinal or organizational partiality that prevents qualified individuals to advance into management level positions.

The glass ceiling keeps women from being promoted equally with men. The glass ceiling has different impacts on men and is often described differently for men: for example, the notion of *hazardous jobs* as a means of dissuading women workers or preventing them from access to specific forms of work (Kimmell, 2000). But women are predominantly the ones who face *the downward spiral*, beginning with motherhood and then maternity leave, which serves often as a huge barrier to promotion.

What really does happen when women enter "men's" occupations and men enter "women's" occupations? In both cases, they experience tokenism. Tokens are accepted not *despite* their minority status but *because of it*. In each instance, workers are actively discouraged from recruiting others like themselves, and become eager to fit in and become part of the organizational mainstream. Typically, tokens may even become more strongly wedded to organizational norms than members of the numerical majority, numerical majority meaning the dominant group of the institution. Kimmel draws on Kanter when stating, "tokenism heightens the boundaries between groups rather than dismantling them, as the contrasts between the token and the majority is exaggerated to become the sole difference" (Kanter cited in Kimmel, 2000). Tokens are treated as representatives of the category or group rather than appreciated for their abilities. Both Zimmer (1998) and Williams (1995) concluded that "men take their gender privilege with them when they enter predominantly female occupations: this translates as an advantage in spite of their numerical rarity. Men seem to win either way." Consequently, when women are tokens, men can retain numerical superiority and are able to maintain their gender privilege, this philosophy restricts a woman's entry, promotion and experiences in the workplace. In this vein, when men are tokens, they are welcomed into the profession, and can use their gender privilege to rise quickly in the hierarchy. Some men may use their gender privilege and some may not, even take a stand for meritocracy. Regardless of the problems that might exist Alfred Kadushin writes

> ...it is clear and undeniable that there is a considerable advantage in being a member of the male minority in any female profession' such as in the education system otherwise known as the male escalator effect in promotion. Some men continue to resist workplace equality, for their privilege is invisible to them. (Kadushin, 1976 cited in Kimmell, 2000)

The factors and barriers that need to be addressed regarding gender positionality in the workplace can be seen as linked to historical circumstances. Historically, social hierarchy has influenced the distribution of material resources, and through these ruling groups has generally attempted to eliminate the thinking and acting capacities of other social positions. Upon this base, elaborate ideologies and theories that legitimate the superiority of some, and the lesser rights and motives of those beneath them have been developed. The labouring classes, especially women, and minority racial and ethnic groups, have all typically faced both restricted access to empowering material resources and degrading portrayals of their inherent intelligence and other abilities as naturally and inevitably diminished (Kimmel, 2000; Livingstone and Sawchuk 2004).

Did the rise of the feminist movement provide or address equality for all the cross-sections of difference that gender embodies? There is an apparent assumption that feminist thought at large is necessarily inclusive of the positions, needs or desires of the minority feminist. I would like to distinguish the two, and point out that at earlier periods of theoretical development and still today in practice, the feminist movement is not necessarily the voice of marginalized minority women. As Ross (1987) points out visible minority women are hardly alone in their protests that the women's movement does not adequately represent their interests and concerns. Women who have no desire to climb the corporate ladder, to secure academic tenure, to hold down "non traditional" jobs, rural and older women have also felt excluded from the feminist promises (Ross, 1987). But the mirror these women hold up to these institutions when trying to gain access to key positions of power in education administration reflects not just feminist thought but moreover, the overwhelming picture of the politics of difference (Bulmer & Solomos, 2004).

Patricia Hill Collins (2000), Bell Hooks (1998) and Njoki Nathani Wane (2002) focused their research on global contexts involving race, feminism and other sociological perspectives. Patricia Hill Collins (2000), who coined Black feminist thought, has addressed the notion of the interlocking matrix of domination as responsive to human agency in terms of gender, race and class, and uses this to analyze all of the social barriers that exist for minority-identified women. She exposes the interconnectedness of the education system and the social barriers faced by minority women in the educational work field. This kind of insight is what decision-makers in the system need to be informed about. Wane (2002) believes this is accomplished by developing visible minorities and feminist epistemological practices that emphasize the importance of all histories, developing critical consciousness and decolonizing our minds. Both Collins and Wane can thus be effectively coupled with research about organizational change, to assist the examination of how minoritized females inform professional mobility.

Miller (1983) advocates for feminist engagement within institutions, that aims to promote change within existing bureaucratic structures. Miller claims there are four structural aspects in organizations that stand out as perpetuating gender inequality: the valuing of heroic individualism, the split between work and family, exclusionary power, and the monoculture of instrumentality. From Acker's (1990) work, it is clear that the gendering of organizations occurs according to "job patterning, the creation of symbols and myths, interactions that entrench dominance and subordination, and the determination of gender-appropriate behaviors and attitudes."

> The *gender lens* was created to interrogate these organizational cultures in terms of equity and women in the workplace.

Acker's work has dealt with gender and teachers' work, but another related body of work has focused on the class position of teachers (Parkin, 1971; Ozga & Lawn, 1981; Wright, 1985; Hatcher, 1994; Carter, 1997; Maguire, 2001). Ball (2003) reflects "on ways in which class works as an identity and a lifestyle, and a set of perspectives on the social world and relationships in it." However, while identities may well be fluid, shifting and socially constructed, material conditions of inequality are durable and persistent. (Lucey & Reay, 2000) While institutional neutrality, objectivity and liberal organizational practices are an attempt to mask and justify discrimination, they are unsuccessful. The marginalization of women is not so benign or direction-less:

These punishing effects of discrimination for women and other minorities is worsened through a variety of micro-inequalities such as: denying the status and authority of women and minorities; devaluing women through sexist comments, anecdotes and "jokes"; excluding or impairing access to information; signaling women's lesser importance through words, behaviours, posture, tone and gestures which indicate that women are not as powerful, intelligent or competent as men and therefore do not need to be taken seriously, these behaviours and practices constitute a chilly climate (Prentice, 2000).

> The backdrop of gender inequality in the valuing of heroic individualism, the split between work and family, exclusionary power, the monoculture of instrumentality and maternity leave seen as impediments within bureaucratic structures are the mitigating factors that drives this study forward in terms of social difference and promotion.

Gender discriminatory practice and male privilege underpins many themes in this study.

> On the other hand, Warren Farrell cited in Kimmel (2000) who argues "that all the attention to the ways women are held back from promotion by the glass ceiling hides that fact that it is men who are the victims of sex discrimination in the workplace. Men are victims of the *glass cellar*, stuck in the most hazardous and dangerous of jobs i.e. safety inspectors, daycare or school board construction workers, etc.)"

There is also a disproportionate amount of male elementary teachers to female. There is a need for more male teachers in the elementary school system to assist closing the achievement gap for boys and all students.

This was the overview of gender issues that inform the study. Florence Abena Dolphyne creates a context for us of the historical significance of the emancipation of women in an African perspective. This will lead us to see the connections between historical gender roles to the present, and take into account how these roles have evolved.

The Emancipation of Women – A Ghanaian Perspective

Florence Abena Dolphyne, Ghanaian social theorist, argues that the emancipation of women differs within the feminist movement because the emancipation has to be considered within a cultural context of practices and traditions. This cultural context helps us to examine how this emancipation practice manifests within education, professional or vocational training that was needed to make young women economically independent. However, Dolphyne pointed out that frequent childbearing is central to cultural tradition.

> This tension of wanting to be an educated professional, be economically sound and have the respect of cultural tradition in frequent childrearing put African women on the defensive for this debate.

Despite the evolution of female professionals in education, Dolphyne tried to explain the complexity of deeply rooted frequent child-bearing traditions have religious and cultural significance in such societies yet have caused high rates of illiteracy and pose career and education attainment barriers. She pointed out

> ...that as educated African women, they realize that the principles underlying these practices are no longer tenable and they fully appreciate the need to work towards the total eradication of such practices. However, what was needed most at this time, when most of the affected societies have a very high proportion of non-literate population living in rural areas, was education to make them aware for improvement of living conditions which will lower infant mortality, one major reason for frequent child-bearing in African women. (Dolphyne, 1991)

Dolphyne (1991) goes on to argue that

> ...women's education has always lagged behind that of men in all African societies, and there are several reasons for this. It has been

explained that in traditional society, a major role for a woman is to ensure the continuity of the lineage, and she was expected to marry soon after puberty. She did not need formal education to perform this function.

Moreover, in return for her labour at home a woman was expected to be provided for by her husband. It was considered more important for boys to have formal education, since they were to be the breadwinners in the family. Dolphyne thinks that in general, it is fairly easy for a girl with no formal education to make a living out of retail or sale of snacks to workers. On account of this traditionally, most girls who started school did not continue beyond the primary school level. When a female does gain access to higher education, it demonstrates many gender barriers to success in the workplace, many based on barriers in attaining education. At the same time, in Ghana today, it is possible to become an educator with a high school diploma, even though a Bachelor's degree is desired.

This Ghanaian cultural context of women, education, work and family has many limiting implications on promotion and addressing it requires cultural and historical contextualization. Dolphyne's work informs this study by adding to an understanding of the parameters within which many Ghanaian women operate. This gives a context to the barriers many aspiring female educators as well as the challenges educational leaders face. Rao, Stuart and Kelleher give us the Western context of historical and present, gender and feminist theory.

Gender Leadership - Western Context

Rao, Stuart and Kelleher (1999), British, American and Canadian researchers, suggest that the premise that the problem of gender inequality is rooted in the institutional arrangements of organizations, which in turn produce gender-inequitable outcomes. Advocates of organizational gender equity often have focused on employment-equity issues such as reducing barriers to women in the workplace and improving the representation of women at higher levels of organizations. Organizations will not become gender equitable without such transformation. Even if powerful leaders wanted equity, the staff was in agreement, and outside constituents were demanding it, current ways of understanding organizations will entrench the status quo. They assert that "trying to *add gender* into the structure and work of organizations is like trying to add the idea that the world is round to the idea that the world is flat." (Rao, Stuart and Kelleher, 1999)

This incompatibility shows the necessity for transformation in incremental and revolutionary changes for gender in organizations. To do this, it is important to look at how power dynamics surrounds organizational gender issues.

> Rao, Stuart and Kelleher (1999) outline six types of distinctive gender leadership.
> 1. Positional Power
> 2. Exclusionary Power
> 3. Agenda-setting Power
> 4. Hidden Power
> 5. Power of Dialogue
> 6. Power of Conflict

Positional power is the authority resulting from an office or title in an organization. *Exclusionary power* works in two ways; if we presuppose that power is a limited commodity, I can have more while you have less. Or there is the opposite approach that power is infinite, and the more we have the more there is. Power-as-energy is the product not only of position but also of information, relationships, and spirit. It focuses on building relationships and the capacity of both individuals and groups to respond to changing organizational and external realities. *Agenda-setting* is another form of power involving an understanding of how the restriction of certain 'taboo' topics can lead to inequity. *Hidden power* is when power is being exercised at the expense of others without their knowledge. For example, hidden power operates in the form of unquestioned assumptions about work practices. And it works as well to maintain an inequitable system. *Power of dialogue* can unearth the exercise of power and expose how it builds or prevents equity. This kind of power can combat elements like informal networks that limit access to privileged information that translates to promotional and career acuity. "Political knitting" describes the information sharing and feedback seeking, as well as problem-solving that is noted above. *Power of conflict* is using confrontational strategies to bind the power of outside pressure and legislation to re-shape the organization. These strategies are a mixture of alliance building, dialogue and pressure tactics (Rao, Stuart & Kelleher, 1999). This kaleidoscope of the many aspects of power is built on the notion that people can strategically engage in (or counter-act) different forms of power-practices. Together, they expose the silent and overt range of forms that power takes within an organization. Some forms of power in this context are particularly relevant to issues of career mobility.

The power of conflict is a double-edged sword. Confrontational behaviours can produce work avoidance. By not wanting to engage another staff member in a disagreement, a person may simply avoid situations where she has to expend energy clashing with a co-worker or boss. However, if not dealt with through avoidance, the power of conflict can be felt through the confrontational conversations, which in some cases may serve as a catalyst for change. Hidden power may be a particularly relevant theme for minority women navigating career progression. By maintaining the invisibility of assumptions about an individual's work or information relevant to it, the space whereby others are left unknowing and insecurity is fostered.

These feminist theories of power have shed light on the unexpected and unique ways of exercising power and leadership, and its limits and possibilities within an organizational context. I argue that people hoping to engage in career progression must recognize and contend with these practices of positional, exclusionary, agenda-setting, dialogue, conflict and hidden power. The relationship of power and privilege in gender (as well as marginalized) occupational roles is central to this study.

Social Difference - Race and Gender Data

RACE

In this section on race, we will examine three main aspects: (1) race neutrality and ethnic nepotism, (2) the community of power versus the dominant group; and synonymous groups of minorities and interview bias, and (3) *community of power* allies and benefits of professional networks in ethnic groups. It is divided in two sub-sections to explore the differences in the Canadian respondents and then, the Ghanaian respondents. Descriptors are given in this section for context purposes for both Ghana and Canada. I also look at the distinctions between tokenism and affirmative action policies, representation and meritocracy issues, and try to take a holistic look at agency in the systems in terms of race in each country.

Canadian Data

The saliency of race in Canada takes on many different shades and displays ripple effects within every day contexts within schools and its boards. There are many different frameworks for understanding the implications of race in Ontario such as multiculturalism, anti-racist education, pluralism, diversity, cultural proficiency, racism and discrimination, etc. Each assumes a certain perspective on issues and has unique points of emphasis. I focused my data collection in diverse populations in the province of Ontario. However, we must ask: do our school leaders and educators reflect this diversity in population? While other sources such as Statistics Canada or school board demographic data can be used to document the facts of under-representation of minorities, here I will draw on the data from my study to explore the research questions raised by this study.

Tony (a middle-aged, Caucasian Italian-Canadian principal with a graduate degree), Linda (a middle-aged, Caucasian Canadian principal with a graduate degree) and Oliver (a middle-aged, Caucasian Canadian principal) see race as neutral. Tony states "I don't see ethnicity and I don't see race as an impediment or a positive – it's neutral, we accept everyone." Linda, "with my experience of the process being on both sides of the desk, being the interviewee and an interviewer, there's no bias in terms of the ethnic or racial background of the person applying." An observation that can be further made is that all three respondents who believe that race is neutral, also presupposes that the power in general is neutral. The *community of power* in this sense is seen through the over-representation of one racial group across the offices of Director of Education, superintendents, principals and vice-principals within Ontario. There are some qualified individuals who are visible minorities who are denied, delayed or alienated access to such leadership positions in education as Vivian (a middle aged, Visible- Minority Caribbean-Canadian principal) spoke about "the backlash she got" when attempting promotion. On this basis, one can question the neutrality in career mobility process, and in fact several of the respondents from the *community of power* or Caucasian principals felt uncomfortable with the term *dominant group* in the interview.

Oliver is part of the community of power, yet has a hearing disability, and believes that race is neutral. He claims "the fact that I am deaf shows that they do have a very equitable hiring policy. Everyone is treated the same." This contradiction was brought on by extrapolating a single experience to be an expression of broader dynamics is, in fact, not unusual in this data. The assumption of the neutrality of power, and the barriers facing minority women educators may even be invisible for those who are visible minorities and women themselves when they draw narrowly on simply their own personal experience. Jasmind (a middle-aged, Visible-Minority Egyptian-Canadian principal) is one in about forty administrators in her school board. She thinks policies are equitable in her board. "It's truly one main initiative – that is equal access to all. I think I am a really good example of that and not only myself."

However, Paul (a middle-aged, Caucasian third generation Canadian principal with a graduate degree) draws on a range of personal experiences and communications with others:

> ...have you had that opportunity to work and there have been barriers to you? Have you felt if you spoke up about issues of race, for example, that you wouldn't be listened to and you felt that would hinder you? Everybody can say they're multicultural and say they are open-minded until somebody says but what about this? I have talked to my colleagues of other ethnic backgrounds, I know they work hard. I grieve the fact that if they've had an experience where they've felt they've had to and they've been held back-that's a terrible thing. I can't pretend it may not have happened. I do know administrators who certainly say we need to have staff that reflects the face of the community. So I'll tell you in my view when I work at this school, I am looking for people of diverse backgrounds...if these kids don't have examples of folks from their kinship circles in education, why would they go into this? When I look amongst my colleagues, I know it is lacking. I've also worked with kids who were a bit marginalized, we worked very hard to convince a lot of these students that they need to go on and get into education, further education. I'm really proud that a number of them went on and have become teachers now. I think it's one of the better triumphs that we've had and they know what they had to do to overcome some of these obstacles. That is the best part of education – liberating people and helping them explore their potential."

Paul's broader orientation and broader sources of information, it would appear, have provided him some deeper insights. He literally attempts to walk in a minority educators' shoes interviewing colleagues to understand the struggle of visible minorities in terms of education promotion. Paul reinforces the need to have greater visible minority representation in school leadership and allies with visible minority educators and current principals. Likewise Shannon (a middle-aged, Caucasian Irish-Canadian principal with a graduate degree) explains:

> what I'm seeing now are children from those different backgrounds becoming young adults and fortunately deciding to choose careers

in education and that means we now have the role models in our classrooms for children seeing people who look like them as the teacher-that gives them a role model to build on. I'm hoping that those young teachers will choose a career in administration so that they can be promoted and be leading schools within a community.

While 'choosing a career in administration' may not be as simple as she supposes, Shannon seeks to ally with visible minority students and educators, and understands the need for higher visible minority representation in classrooms and in leading school communities. Peter (a middle-aged, Caucasian British-Canadian principal) believes a step forward happened with his school board community,

> ...there was a survey last year with the whole staff on race and ethnicity that we were all asked to take part in. Whether you were an educational assistant, a teacher, a principal, you were asked to take part in it and what they're looking at doing there is tracking promotionability. Where you watch somebody from the time they become a teacher to the time they became a director and you're looking at that information based on their background, their race, their ethnicity-those kinds of factors...whether or not, they do play a role and whether or not minority groups are getting promoted or not.

While empathy and moving beyond narrow experiences is important, Peter's comments above nevertheless underline an important dynamic when he outlines his solution: it leaves the power to bring about systemic change exclusively in the hands of current administration, well intentioned and otherwise.

Ghanaian Data

Both Mensa (a middle-aged, Twi-Ashanti head master with Ghana Education Service credentials) and Yvonne (a middle-aged, Twi-Akwapim head mistress with Ghana Education Service credentials) are from dominant ethnic groups. The dominant group of Twi-Akwapim which is the second largest ethnic representation after Twi-Ashanti, but they each have something distinct to say about the race, ethnicity and the promotion issue. Mensa believes "in Ghana here, we're all Ghanaian - as one nation - so we don't value racial discrimination. I am Ashanti and I've been working in Ashanti land." Yvonne however speaks to "some ethnic nepotism exists because when you get your own person, where you come from, the same racial [background], they favour you." Ethnic nepotism operates in terms of family or blood line. If you are from the same ethnic background in some situations you have privileged access in promotion. The Ashanti ethnicity in Ghana is the *community of power* or the critical mass *dominant group*. Most of the education dignitaries are from the Ashanti ethnicities, the minority groups, Ewe and Ga ethnicities have much smaller numbers in representation of educators and school principals in the education system.

Besides racial or ethnic nepotism in the hiring process, there is another area to investigate, the application process. Nii (a middle-aged, mixed ethnic origin of Twi-Ashanti and Ga head master with Ghana Education Service credentials) asserts, "on the application, there's no column to check your ethnicity but in the interview, they will ask you to describe something about yourself and where you were born and that indicates to them what area and what ethnicity you are from…there are ways of finding out that information." Nala (a middle-aged, Twi-Ashanti ethnic origin head mistress with a university degree) discusses informal ethnic professional networks. The Ashanti-Twi, Ewe and Ga ethnicities have their own professional networks but they also come together and meet in a mixed ethnicity network at times. Nala explains "we have mixture of ethnicities, it helps me. Not just Ashanti-Twi or Ga but all ethnicities. We discuss what ethnicities are missing a place, what some ethnicities are not doing or are doing good elements…it may encourage some change and make aware of missing people [or ethnicities]" in education. The conscious discussions highlighting strengths and areas of improvement within the *community of power* in formalized professional networks around *ethnicism* issues in education. This brings the potential for a healthy awareness to address the serious issues such as representation of minority ethnicities and the like. The development of mixed professional networks, in turn, allows the broader sharing of cultural knowledge allowing those from subordinate ethnic origins to build capacities for career progression.

GENDER

In this section on gender, we will examine three main aspects: (1) historical impact of male dominated school leadership and the old boys' network, (2) contrast of women heading the entire education system and its impact, (3) family-work balance in promotion and teacher replacement problem on maternity leaves. It is divided in two sub-sections to explore the differences in the Canadian respondents and then, the Ghanaian respondents. I have included descriptors for the respondents for context and identity intersectional purposes. I look at the distinctions between feminist and anti-feminist attitudes, cases of males supporting women in their careers, the impact of dissenters, and how the *glass ceiling* and *sticky floor* models, as well as the *male escalator* effect takes place across both countries.

Canadian Data

There are remnants of gender, power and politics that are still vividly at play today that create the silent sting of the imbalance of power. Carol (a middle-aged, Caucasian British-Canadian female principal with a graduate degree) understands very well that:

> the old boys' network is alive and well. There is opportunity but I think you might have to go a little bit further out to find it—if you're not aligned with anybody in the old boys' network sadly... [You have to] make sure you have a voice and there are enough people out there who are willing to listen to you to lend you credence by acknowledging its existence but sometimes it's not a good thing and your career will take a backseat...by rocking the boat.

Giselle's (a middle-aged, Caucasian Canadian female principal with a graduate degree) experience mirrors Carol's opinion that "the old boys network exists." Sean (a middle-aged, Caucasian Canadian male principal with a graduate degree) shares "when I was a lad going to school – to be principal, you had to be a male teacher with a number of years and that was it." Jasmind (a middle-aged, Visible-Minority Egyptian-Canadian female principal) discloses "a few years ago, the promotions for principals were more male than female...the history of this school if you look at all the principals – they were all male. I'm the first female." Marina (a mature-aged, Caucasian Canadian female principal) agrees "historically, becoming a school administrator was a lot harder. There was never even a consideration about a woman becoming a principal. It was strictly a male domain. I cannot even think of one female principal that was around when I started teaching...the culture has totally changed." Cynthia (a mature-aged, Caucasian Canadian female principal) sheepishly admits "my Dad was an elementary school principal but he was chosen. Those days the avenues were demarcated for certain groups of people."

Women gaining access to school leadership has a deep rooted past, as in the case of race. Historically, men were appointed or hand-picked to become a school leader. It was inconceivable for another option. Cynthia, it seemed gained an internal understanding where she realized it was not that long ago that this systemic behaviour happened because this is how her father was chosen. This connects to Jasmind, looking around the room at the picture of the past principals of the school as she realizes or embraced that she was the first female. Conversations also concretized the realities of gender politics still at play today. There was an acknowledgment that '*the club door*' often had no key for women, the old boys' network still exists and its exclusionary nature permeates through the school leadership culture throughout school boards. It needs to be under-scrutiny, the *glass ceiling* needs to be brought to the forefront so it can be absolved and the awareness of the *male escalator* in school promotion also needs to heightened. Sean understands the *glass ceiling* that still exists for women in school leadership, he states:

> if I look at the number of administrators still in our school board in the elementary panel – it still does not reflect the gender bias of elementary educators who – 90% are women but well over 90% of principals are not women - in our board it's well over 50% in our area but that's not reflected in the administration and the same is with ethnic variety for want of a better term in administration… it's not reflective of community.

Sean brings to bare the gender representation problem as Dwayne (a middle-aged, Visible-Minority Jamaican-Canadian male principal with a graduate degree) does in terms of lack of race representation.

The second issue in career mobility is the *family versus promotion* dilemma. Again, Paul (a middle-aged, Caucasian, third generation Canadian male principal with a graduate degree) addresses this issue with awareness and empathy:

> I think women have to be thinking a little bit more about when to do this and how to do this and what commitment can they make to their position versus to their families and that's not to say that men don't have responsibilities to families as well, it will work itself out a little differently…I will tell you though I know some women who are superior administrators and they're also obviously superior at being able to raise children and I think in fact ironically having a family is an opportunity to become a better teacher and administrator.

This echoes Jasmind's opinion on *the family factor*. Marina (a mature-aged, Caucasian Canadian female principal) and Vivian (a middle-aged, Visible-Minority Caribbean-Canadian female principal with a graduate degree) acknowledge the disadvantages of maternity leave on a female's career. Marina states "many women decide to have children so there are breaks in their careers." Vivian adds maternity is an impediment because "you're out of the loop, you are going to be that many paces behind everybody else when you come back."

There are three broad themes that emerge:
(1) The first is the presence of the old boys' network now and in history.
(2) The second is the disproportionate ratio of majority female elementary teachers to the lack of representation in positions of school leadership.
(3) The third is the family question in career mobility.

Historically, the respondents both men and women were in agreement that men had for the most part sole access to promotion. Now, there are entry-points and openings for women; however, the power dynamics of the old boys' networks are still at play. The family factor that the respondents discuss is a positive double-edge sword. This oxymoron is that having a child, female educators tacit knowledge increases parenting, caretaking, health care and a plethora of informal skills that are gained. However, the practical issues that was apparent where a maternity leave creates an education-work gap of staying current and abreast of changes and initiatives within your school board. Maternity and child-rearing could also postpone a female educator's career for years but ambition can circumvent further career delay.

Ghanaian Data

In this particular area in Ghana, Koforidua has made many recent strides in women's school leadership roles. Emmanuel (a mature-aged, Ga ethnic origin head master with a university degree) believes this is attributed to:

> in Ghana, they like the person who is in authority, the regional director currently is a woman. So, they make most of the heads women. They think women are better administrators. They take good care of money. They think women will do better than the men because of the bias of those in authority appointing more women than men.

Yvonne (a middle-aged, Twi-Akwapim ethnic origin head mistress with Ghana Education Service credentials) offers an alternative explanation to this argument by stating "women are put in a high position. We are able to manage the position well." Selwin (a middle-aged, Ga ethnic origin head master with Ghana Education Service credentials) agrees with her and states "women are more careful with their work in Ghana than men." Angelina (a middle-aged, Twi-Akwapim ethnic origin head mistress with Ghana Education Service credentials) thinks "women plan differently from their male counterparts because there are certain jobs that are meant for women." Nii (a middle-aged, mixed ethnic origin Twi-Ashanti and Ga head master with Ghana Education Service credentials) takes an objective standpoint of a policy; there is a "gender equity policy...that one is based on the number of people who apply, we give room for both male and female."

Clearly, there are certain sentiments of feminist or anti-feminist emotional and thought processes here. The balance or imbalance between policies and the political gender undercurrent of the system are both important for understanding the interactions at play in the hiring process. It seems as though competition versus cooperation arises, but support for women comes from all different people. There are males that support females and are very vocal in their convictions. The dissenters believe it is the sign of the times and are anxiously awaiting the tide to turn again to the male dominant system of order. The polarity of position within gender and promotion in Ghana leads me to believe, more political interaction and educational leadership interplay will continue for years to come.

The issue of family-work balance and maternity take on a culturally specific reference in the Ghanaian data. Nala (a middle-aged, Twi-Ashanti head mistress with a university degree) states in this society:

> a woman needs to marry or has to marry and all that we expect from marriage is children, so the moment you get married in my area here and there's no children-they tend to fool about especially the men and the family of the man will not respect you, the woman. They will make a mockery of you...teachers go on maternity and tend to look at this area first than go for a promotion once the home and family life is settled...I am proud to say 80% of women are heading schools these days in Ghana.

Ado (a middle-aged, mixed ethnic origin Ewe and Ga head master with a university degree) explains, this is due to the fact, that many men are leaving the education field and are going into more lucrative fields such as business. The fact that having children is the value-glue that holds many Ghanaian families together, moreover, the more children you give back to the family the better the relation is. This is problematic to the aspiring Ghanaian career woman.

Other barriers exist for her expressed by Rose (a middle-aged, Twi-Ashanti ethnic origin head mistress with Ghana Education Service credentials) and Selwin (a middle-aged, Ga ethnic origin head master with Ghana Education Service credentials). They state experiencing teacher replacement problems during women's maternity at their school. Rose explains

> ...maternity does cause some problems because currently we don't have replacements... [This] is not a Ministry service. For example, if there are 10 to 15 women going on maternity in the area, there may only be 5 people to replace them. So, the other schools have to manage their own areas, how to be able to cater in their absence and they have to rely on their heads to fill in the teaching gaps... this is a problem, if I have meetings outside school children's learning is neglected.

In other areas and schools, Asenso (a middle-aged, Twi-Ashanti ethnic origin head master with a university degree) says "it is valued because maternity leaves are given to women. We have two women on maternity leave and it doesn't go against them at all; it counts as service worked." This is a progressive response to be emulated, but it seems that the maternity/teacher replacement issue depends upon the school, its location and its availability in terms of human capital resources or supply teachers from the school board. There is a shortage of school board funding, thus there is a lack of teacher supply. This remains a perpetual problem in some schools. We now turn toward yet another missing piece to the puzzle of career mobility found in a discussion of Gary Becker's notion of human capital, Robert Putnam's notion of social capital, and Pierre Bourdieu's notion of cultural capital.

Chapter 4

Rapids Educators Engender Swimming Upstream

[Professionals] with higher levels of cultural and social capital are more likely to be placed in more intellectually demanding roles and functions. This experience, in turn, can have positive effect in the expansion of their social and cultural capital, and eventually their transferability to economic capital e.g. higher employability.

(Schugurensky and Mundel, 2005)

For the purpose of this study, I just wanted to take a moment to briefly introduce a few terms that are central to the discussion later on. The terms *cultural* and *social capital* are pertinent to examine the dynamics between structure and agency in the reproduction of social inequality. The quote above suggests the importance of the distinction between these two forms of capital. In the previous chapters, I also used the term *human capital*.

By way of a brief orientation to these terms: this study refers to human capital as the process of educational credential attainment/accumulation; social capital refers to the accumulation of contacts within a social network (e.g. a school system); and, cultural capital is understood as the accumulation of knowledge relevant to a particular cultural system which is typically organized to privilege some forms of (race, gender, class, etc.) cultural knowledge over others.

Recognition of each of these factors contributes to understanding the possibilities and limitations that the factors of human, social and cultural capital create regarding the kinds of social relationships that bear on a potential candidate's progress. In light of these concepts, I would like to take a closer look at the factors of social status, values and disposition, individual capital, learning strategies, knowledge base and skill-gaps in relation to career advancement in the data set. Class will be a relevant factor in examining the effects of geography, race, post-colonial remnants and gender practice. Keeping in mind the latter, I will now explore career mobility, leadership, agency attribute and the human, social and cultural capital practices, and discuss the relevance of social relationships as valued in career mobility as well as individual knowledge and skill advocacy. I will be applying these ideas to the data to develop a stronger, more interactive and multi-mediational understanding of career mobility in education across the data from two contexts (Ghana and Canada).

Examining the different factors (human, social and cultural capital accumulation) I attempt to show how they interact with each other to shape an educator's journey as she attempts to advance professionally. Moreover, carrying out this analysis allows us the opportunity for important international comparative dimension to the findings which tells us more about each national context than would otherwise be possible. While all three forms of capital may be at play, will some be more important than others? Can a minoritized educator navigate a successful track to promotion considering the embedded, interactive barriers in the system? How large is the role of social difference in including or excluding one who is being considered for promotion? The thirty respondents' thoughts, stories, testimonials and learning associated with career mobility are multi-faceted and complex. To address this line of questioning, we will first explore the fifteen Canadian respondents' interviews then the fifteen Ghanaian respondents in a comparative format.

With this context in mind, the material in this chapter is informed by the following objectives:
1. To what extent, and how do the Ghanaian and Canadian respondents overlap in ideology and practice?
2. What agency attributes emerge for Canada and Ghana? How is the researcher going to separate the qualifiable and quantifiable attributes, and how does this inform the analysis?
3. How does race and gender materialize in their different international contexts, what learning could we gain from the findings?
4. What is (are) the dominant form(s) of capital that explains career mobility in the countries in the study?

This review of career mobility, leadership and social difference theory within an educational context will reflect on a range of theorists who have explored their relationship to structural change and personal empowerment. This relationship is like a pendulum, at one end of the spectrum are theorists who advocate for structural change; and on the other end are those who put forth hypotheses that allow for personal autonomy in the actor's own unique, cultural settings. Moreover, there are many theorists who have culturally attuned models and begin with collectivism and others who purport individualism and agency.

Why is their unequal representation in education promotional opportunities of school leadership? This kind of question of social inequity has preoccupied many sociology theorists over the past few decades. Drawing some orientation from the work of Robert Putnam (1993; 1995), Gary Becker (1964; 1993; 1994) and Pierre Bourdieu (1973; 1986; 1997; 1998), it can be seen that these theorists analyze how social inequity manifests, reproduces and sustains itself in systems to maintain unequal power relations perpetually. Social difference disadvantages rooted in jobs, careers and promotions are in line with many of the arguments offered by these theorists. Most people think attaining *higher education* would equalize this factor but enhancing one's human capital does not necessarily mean one will attain a job at the level of his or her qualifications, or still may not have access to certain jobs due to other systemic barriers.

The three very different forms of capital (human, social and cultural capital) express both the structural and individual dimensions.

> Together, these different *capital accumulation* processes illuminate the processes that individual engage in terms of educational credential obtainment, social networks participation, and culturally specific forms of knowledge.

But, these three forms of capital also have embedded within them structural consequences and meaning: an individual's accumulation of any type of capital takes on significance in relation to existing organizational or society institutions or structures. Occupational aspirations for promotion, as a mediating link between socioeconomic structures and individuals, play a crucial role in systemic reproduction of inequality in the career promotional system within the field of education. At the interface between structural determinants and human agency, aspirations offer the sociologist a conceptual bridge over the theoretical cleft of structure-agency.

HUMAN, SOCIAL AND CULTURAL CAPITAL LITERATURE
Three Forms of Capital-How Social Differences are Translated into Hierarchies of Career Opportunity

Human Capital: Becker

*the investment of education, training and skill-based learning of an individual is argued to have a greater return on investment in the form of future professional endeavours.

Social Capital: Putnam

*refers to connections among individuals-social networks and the norm of reciprocity and trustworthiness that arise from them.

Cultural Capital: Bourdieu

*perpetuates inequality reproduction through hierarchical structures and constitutes cultural background, knowledge, disposition and skills that are passed generationally.

Structural Change and Personal Empowerment in School Promotion: Ghana & Canada

*divergence and convergence in the ideological continuum from structural changes to personal empowerment in terms promotion is critical to see how the study intersects.

*The *Mobility Field* represents the positionality of mobility capital.

Essed (1991), Dolphyne (1991), and Rao, Stuart & Kelleher's (1999) schools of thought each emphasize the importance of human agency in occupational injustice and inequitable situations. We have seen that disparity in educational promotion and having deep aspirations to attain higher school leadership levels; is at the root of the tensions that emerge from Ghanaian and Canadian educators. After we have familiarized ourselves with some of the basic aspects of social reproduction, and career mobility, we are now in a position to examine in depth the mobility field.

The mobility field is the theoretical framework formed by the forms of interaction across human, social and cultural capital. With this context in mind, the material in this chapter is informed by the following objectives:

1. How does the literature outline the relationship between structural change and personal empowerment?
2. What explanation of career mobility can an analysis of human, social and cultural capital provide us with?

Capital and Social Difference - Hierarchies of Career Opportunity

There are three forms of capital that I will investigate. I argue here and later in my analysis that an awareness of these dimensions of work and career mobility extends appreciation of the resources and navigational choices. While the previous section outlines in detail scholarship on, in particular, race and gender differences, power and leadership, to better understand how these interactive factors work together to shape career mobility in education. In particular, we will now look at distinct forms and patterns of (human, social and cultural) capital *accumulation* practices. Each form of capital is mediating the possibilities of the others.

The multi-faceted nature of career mobility is shaped by human, social and cultural capital. Thus, for this study I needed an umbrella framework that has overlapping interconnections. The interactive nature of capital practices is what makes career mobility multi-faceted not the theories. Moreover, capital practices are informed by theory, thus, we can draw upon critical feminist and anti-racist pedagogies in relation to career mobility to see further overlapping connections. Below, I will begin with Gary Becker and human capital, continue with Robert Putnam and social capital, and finally, Pierre Bourdieu and cultural capital and, look at how the dynamics each entails inform issues of race and gender.

After the brief journey of the three dimensions of capital, I will synthesize them into a mobility field. The mobility field attempts to give a historical theoretical backdrop on the three forms of capital where an emerging (career) mobility capital hypothesis could be positioned.

In other words, it is important to note that each capital theory has its distinct definition and position in the mobility field framework: a framework which is intended to bring to mind that each form of capital can shape the others. This framework is rooted in a type of broad, critical career pedagogy.

Can the mobility field framework add to our understanding of how a marginalized educator can become empowered to maneuver vertically in one's career progression?

Human Capital

The basis of the human capital theory is the analogy between physical and human capitals.

> In human capital, the investment of education, training and skill-based learning of an individual is argued to have a greater return on investment in the form of future professional or job-related endeavours pending one's retirement age, higher salaries and better employability.

In the economic theory, human capital is a factor of production identical to labour and physical capital. The human capital theory was created by Theodore Schultz (Schultz, 1961); however, it became popularized by Gary Becker's book "Human Capital" which became the school's main piece of work (1964). Jacob Mincer (1962, 1974) contributed to human capital's popularity by the added earnings function, which is the most important experiential tool of human capital analysis within the school of thought. In addition, human capital has partially different contents on the individual and organizational levels. At the individual level, the flow component of human capital includes conscious investments in human capital in the form of training and education. The conscious component has strong innovation potential and traditional learning accrual has opposing forms of learning. However, after leaving school, these innovative potential components are most frequently exercised in unintentional, spontaneous ways (European Union Ministry of Labour, 2006).

Human capital, as Carnoy and Levin (1985) point out is based on the fact that "schools are driven by the contradictory dynamics of what they [education authorities] call a capitalist imperative and a democratic imperative." Livingstone (1987) argues that "included within the capitalist imperative, for instance, are employers' demands for appropriately disciplined and skilled workers and working-class demands for education and training that will result in meaningful, well-paid employment". The issue of who benefits from education extends beyond class lines, encompassing demands for representation, access, equity and opportunity coming from various groups, including women, visible minorities and others. The intersectionality of one's various social grouping and location is important because access and demand for opportunity creates tension in an already competitive principal or educational leadership job market.

> The intellectual capital of an organization consists of three elements: human capital in personnel, the structural or organizational intellectual capital and customer [or "student"] intellectual capital (Stewart, 1999).

If all the employees left the school board, human capital as well as labour power would disappear, but the structural/organizational intellectual capital, which is independent of the existence of the employees, would remain. It exists in the form of process descriptions, databases, manuals, networks, etc. Organizational learning is the (formal, informal, non-formal and tacit) process in which one creates structural intellectual capital from human capital and other sources. For example, the employees' experiences can be gathered into large databases thus, sustaining the school board's intellectual capital.

A major explanation for that new direction is given by a recent reformulation of human capital theory which has stressed the significance of education and training as the key to participation in the new global economy. In one of its recent reports, the Organisation for Economic Co-operation and Development (OECD, 1997) explains that "internationalization in higher education as a component of globalization". The OECD (1997) for example believes that "internationalism should be seen as a preparation for 21st century capitalism". The organization also boldly asserts that internationalism is "a means to improve the quality of education" (OECD, 1997). In keeping with human capital theory, it has been argued that "the overall economic performance of the OECD countries is increasingly more directly based upon their knowledge stock and their learning capabilities" (Foray & Lundvall, 1996). Clearly, the OECD is trying to produce a new role for education in terms of the human capital required in *globalized* institutions.

There are limits to the human capital theory however. Under this theory, it is inconceivable that human activity viewed as the exchange of commodities and the notion of capital employed is purely a quantitative one. This misses the point that capital is an independent social force where the creation of social value comes about through its capital accumulation and continual change processes through the circulation of commodities (Block, 1990). Arguments about economic growth accounting such as Becker (1994), explains that education in some form contributes to differences in earnings between people and in various circumstances. The discussion surrounding economic growth emanates from education is debatable because, while it may be granted that education contributes to growth, but so do countless other factors. Another economic term that would be useful to this study is *opportunity cost*. Opportunity cost is the cost of passing up the next best choice when making a decision. If we act or don't act on our career mobility, there is a cost every time (i.e. miss a benefit such as a promotion, family factor). Ultimately, every career decision has a cost.

Social Capital

James Coleman, Robert Putnam and Michael Woolcock defined and redefined the meaning of social capital. Coleman expands on his notion of social capital by defining its functions as "it is not a single entity, but a variety of different entities, having two characteristics in common: they all consist of some aspect of a social structure, and they facilitate certain actions of individuals who are within the structure" (Coleman 1994). Putnam (2000) argues:

> ...whereas physical capital refers to physical objects and human capital refers to the properties of individuals, social capital refers to connections among individuals – social networks and the norms of reciprocity and trustworthiness that arise from them. In that sense social capital is closely related to what some have called "civic virtue." The difference is that "social capital" calls attention to the fact that civic virtue is most powerful when embedded in a sense network of reciprocal social relations. A society of many virtuous but isolated individuals is not necessarily rich in social capital.

Coleman's view is more tinged in that he discerns the value of connections for all actors, individual and collective, privileged and disadvantaged. But Coleman's view is also hopeful; as a public good, social capital is almost entirely benevolent in its functions, providing for a set of norms and sanctions that allow individuals to cooperate for mutual advantage and with mention of conflict, sabotage or negative interactions that can arise within social networks, in which Field calls the 'dark side'. (Field, 2003) As Smith (2007) notes:

> Social capital allows citizens to resolve collective problems more easily... People often might be better off if they cooperate, with each doing her share. Social capital greases the wheels that allow communities to advance smoothly...Social capital refers to connections among the individuals, social networks and norms of reciprocity and trustworthiness that arise from them".

The networks that constitute social capital also serve as conduits for the flow of helpful information that facilitates achieving our goals. Michael

Woolcock (2001), a social scientist with the World Bank has distinguished between three social capitals: *bonding social capital* (connections between people in similar situations), *bridging social capital* (encompasses more distant associations with people) and *linking social capital* (ties unlike people in dissimilar situations). All three social capitals have different combinations that produce different outcomes (Field, 2003).

> Social capital is part of the fabric of organizational life and the need to engage with human networking is, exponential with an institutional setting.

Cohen and Prusak (2001) argue the benefits of social capital within organizational settings are "better knowledge sharing, due to established trust relationships, common frames of reference, and shared goals." (Cohen and Prusak, 2001)

Cultural Capital

The theorist most responsible for advancing the term, cultural capital is Pierre Bourdieu. Bourdieu's most significant contribution to reproduction theory is the concept of cultural capital, which he defines as the general cultural background, knowledge, disposition, and skills that are passed from one generation to the next. (Bourdieu, 1973; 1984; 1986; 1998) Cultural capital is the centerpiece of Bourdieu's theory of cultural reproduction. Children of upper-class origin, according to Bourdieu, inherit substantially different cultural capital than do working-class children. If we apply this concept to educators, then educators who inherit upper, middle or working-class cultural knowledge and certain disposition, this will have an impact on their promotional ability within a particularly cultural setting that rewards some but not all. Bourdieu shows that by embodying class interests and ideologies, the school system rewards the cultural capital of the dominant classes and systemically undervalues those in a lower class. (Bourdieu, 1986; MacLeod, 1995)

> This study focuses on cultural capital involved in integrating one's dispositions, past experiences, and perceptions, and so on, into a certain cultural/work environment. As an expression of cultural capital in a person, there is a correlation between objective probabilities and subjective aspirations, between institutional structures and cultural practices.

We see that:

> Aspirations reflect an individual's view of his or her own chances for getting ahead and are an internalization of objective probabilities. But aspirations are not the product of a rational analysis; rather, they are acquired in the habitus of the individual...the habitus functions as a regulator between individuals and their external world, between human agency and social structure. (MacLeod, 1995)

The mechanisms of cultural and social reproduction remain hidden, because the social practices that safeguard the political and economic interests of the dominant classes go unrecognized as anything but natural.

In this line of reasoning, one exercises advantages gained through human capital or being highly educated, but separate from this one's accumulation of the form of cultural capital privileged in a particular work setting also plays a role. Bourdieu's work centers around these types of questions: [w]hat constitutes "knowledge"; how knowledge is to be achieved; how knowledge is validated and so forth, and shows these as expressions of power and ideology. This is fundamental to the social difference and education promotion debate. In particular, we could think about the way powerful groups in our society are able to define these questions and, by so doing, provide their offspring (and those that look and act like their offspring) with cultural as well as career advantages (Smith, 2007).

Important to this study is extending the notion of cultural capital beyond simply issues of the differences between social classes, to include forms of cultural knowledge, dispositions that relate to marginalized, gendered and racialized groups as well. In other words, work organizations privilege specific race and gender cultures as well as class-based ones. In terms of career mobility, this would mean that learning and accumulating the dominant forms of cultural capital (e.g. becoming more like a man, more like the dominant race/ethnicity, more like a middle-class person, etc.) would assist progression to principalship, yet leave the system largely unchanged. Building on this, I would say that it might also mean that in accumulating different forms of cultural capital that are not privileged (e.g. the unique cultural knowledge of a minority woman teacher) can also be an asset to differentiate the kinds of results, initiatives and productivity added to a school board. In this second case, there is a chance of not merely having more minority women in positions of leadership, but also that their own forms of cultural knowledge or capital may be a resource for transforming the system as well.

Looking across the different theories of capital (human, social and cultural) many questions arise. The following questions inform the study: does the school board consider a person's neighbourhood, financial situation and means in regards to promotion? What barriers are there in formalized education and attaining credentials? How does social access of professional networks affect an aspiring educator's chances for mobility? If an educator wants to gain experience as an educator or administrator outside of his or her social-class, would it be encouraged or be another perceived barrier? Are there occupational culture, social difference, language, power, value and cultural custom stigmas or issues that come into questions during the hiring process? These types of questions, I argue, are dealt with by combining the kinds of issues I have reviewed thus far. I do some of this by constructing what I call a *mobility field* framework.

The Three Dimension Mobility Field

The three forms of capital must be seen as mutually constituting (which can be represented through a triangle model that highlights how each affects the other). Combining these types of capital in this way we gain a sense of how *social differences* are converted into *social hierarchies* in relation to career mobility. The mobility field is interdisciplinary. It has sociological, economic, equity studies, organizational development and career theory within its context.

The mobility field framework therefore includes issues of human capital investment: principles of constant educational or professional improvement based on developing skills and knowledge-base to compete for higher positions within an organization. Social capital relates to career mobility in terms of networking and the trust involved in networking. Cultural capital speaks to the nature of social inequalities that exists within a system that is filled with political implications and questions of identity reviewed earlier.

> The three dimensions are fluid, gravitational and mediational; fluid in the sense that it is situational and situations can change; gravitational in the sense that people are drawn to interact with each other; and mediational in the sense that any one dimension mediates the results of the remaining two.

People's career mobility depends on the interaction between, at least, these different types of social processes and resources. The figure below attempts to show the thinking of researchers in relation to each other, in order to explain this. The start at the centre of the figure is meant to signal an analytic position where there is balance across these different dimensions. It is also a symbol of the complex reality of an individual person, or in the case of my research, an educator.

The three capitals, human, social and cultural capital are the basis of the model. I argue, through this mobility field figure, that it is important to note that individual theorists, even foundational theorists, may have contributed to the canvas but cannot complete the picture. In terms of human capital, Becker is positioned as the entry-point or as the root, the beginning necessity to initialize your career and its potential mobility. Informing this root are the Human Resource Management Organization's ladder and Schultz's spiral in career theories: they add nuance to the straight-forward idea that people simply get credentials and then advance.

Three Dimensional Capital: The Mobility Field

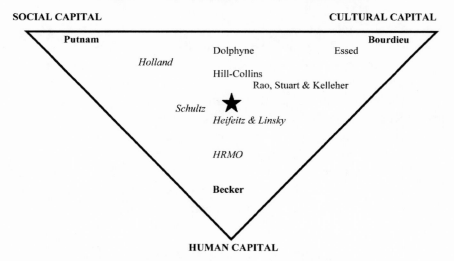

The second capital, the left apex is represented by the work of Putnam: the people skills and community support network arena. Closely related (in the figure, located closer to the social capital / Putnam point) I have positioned the work of Holland's career web theory and Dolphyne's African-feminist theory. This work extends and adds detail to how social networks function and how social differences are involved in them. The third form of capital, the right apex, we see Bourdieu. His work acknowledges systemic social inequality and difference are hierarchically organized. However, we saw that Bourdieu's work needs to be expanded beyond social class issues. Therefore, close to Bourdieu I have placed the work of Essed on the theory of everyday racism. Her work, along with the work of Collins and others on race and gender, help us to apply a more multi-dimensional appreciation for the role of cultural knowledge. The kinds of issues raised in the work of Rao, Stuart & Kelleher which are situated between human and cultural capital, as well as having some relationship to social capital.

As I move into the analysis of data, it will be shown that the mediational approach of the mobility field can be used to compare patterns of practice within the lives of individual educators, as well as between educational administrators in Ghana and Canada. I hope to show that any single form of *capital accumulation* does not account for the whole of people's career mobility process. The attainment of credentials, for example, must be accompanied by attention to social networking; social networking is dependent on micro and macro politics of cultural knowledge within a school or school system; and yet, gaining access to either social networks or different forms of cultural knowledge is dependent on having the credentials to become a teacher and then a principal. All are deeply shaped by issues of race, gender and power.

Interactive Capital Data

In this section examining the different factors of human, social and cultural capital, we will examine three main aspects: (1) credentialism, and the four different types of learning including formal, informal, non-formal and tacit knowledge, (2) credibility and respect in school board community, and community networks based on good working relationships, and (3) the need for ethnic, visible minority and gender representation, the use of the *language of power* and the need to build allies in the *dominant groups* and agency of political and social savvy. As outlined previously, human capital refers to personal investment in one's own education, social capital is an investment in one's relationships and influence with others within one's organization and cultural capital refers to how social differences are hierarchically organized in terms of cultural knowledge. This section has two sub-sections in each section to explore the differences in the Canadian respondents and then, the Ghanaian respondents.

I explore the advantages and disadvantages of certain forms of capital in terms of career mobility in school administration in each country. This section on different forms of capital poses important questions. Which teacher candidate would appear to have greater competence, one who has the savvy to gain more valuable social capital through strong relationships with other influential stakeholders including senior school and board management or one who has the credentials which determine the opportunities for success? In other words, to what extent, does social, human and cultural capital play a role in explaining the outcomes of social differences which, in turn help us to understand barriers for education practitioners in career mobility? How do discourses on social status or disposition, organizational power, professional development, and learning strategies, either sustain promotional leadership or oppressive occupational practices? The respondents' teased out some of these answers in their responses as they grappled with the questions.

HUMAN CAPITAL

Canadian Data

In Canada, growing levels of educated professionals are investing in higher education. They are attaining higher qualifications. This has tended to produce an education-job gap (Livngstone 2004), where the demand for a promotion is high, and the amount of qualified or over-qualified education professionals is in a surplus. But the good news is: the forecast is that the tide is turning. Not unlike in the case of Ghana, an individual can circumvent this by transferring to another school board or changing geographical locations where positions in school administration are high.

The focus for human capital is credentialism. As Tony explained, "I tried to prepare myself by attaining the credentials that were necessary in order to make the application." Oliver believes "education is your number one stepping stone" and Peter states "academic status" is the key to success. Paul experienced the principal-ship as "a continual learning adventure." Vivian supports this by stating "continually learning, striving and growing, never feeling as though they've arrived but always working towards something, getting better-becoming more skilled, becoming more proficient and so I think that you can become much more skilled in your level of competence, professional development...keep learning." Jasmind reminds us that

...the only thing that I can think of for economical or financial restraints are the necessity to take courses to upgrade – that could impede a few people along the way although I know that grants and loans happen a lot more now. Our board has been very good at sponsoring people for courses i.e. Special Education, ESL, French or others that the board needs...but it might be a little bit of a hindrance.

In general, the Canadian respondents did not speak to formal education or human capital as elaborately as Ghanaians did. Yet credentialism, attaining your qualifications is perceived as a given in order to be promoted in Canada. Jasmind problematize the attainment process of courses and degrees pertaining to its financial restraints; however, we have access to grants, loans, scholarships, bursaries, fellowships, and have flexible programming and school-work options. The background is lifelong learning, attaining additional courses specifically, a Principal Qualifications Program (PQP), Part I and II in the province, and continual upgrading. The foreground is the credential and degree that is mandated and standard in each school board before you even apply.

Ghanaian Data

In addition to the types of structured intellectual capital, progression through the rank system discussed earlier, *formal* learning is important in broader ways as well. For example, Selwin states "you have to be a certified A teacher, have extra certificates like O levels and A levels or a university degree...their qualifications." Asenso knows you "must be a university graduate, a BA holder." There are different ways of attaining the degree. A creative program Asenso described was the sandwich program "they work on the job and then in June, July and August, they go to the university campus." It is a higher education alternative but "the fees are so high and income levels are so low, it detracts a lot of people from attaining their degrees." Bettina mentions the sandwich program as well. Yvonne states the "middle and upper class have an advantage because now a days, university education is very costly and if you don't have the money-you can't go." Loans, bursaries and grants are not common practice in tertiary education in Ghana; there is limited or no access in some cases. Emmanuel believes "if you have an additional degree or diploma, you have advantage over all other candidates." He feels it is important to understand "how to use human capital to enhance your school by "raising the academic standard in school and also by having ambitions to head large schools." Nii understands that "qualifications-education wise you should attain some degree...but someone might be a degree holder, MA holder but cannot deliver."

In terms of *non-formal* learning credentials, Asenso says "teachers and principals go to some workshops or special in-services to learn the ins and outs of the work before any new position" or rank. Yvonne articulates there are some but in her opinion, "there needs to be more working sessions before qualified to be a principal...teachers are pursuing many courses." Mensa thought it was important to attend "remedial classes organized by the Ghana Education Service...they provide tests before interviews."

Informal and *tacit* learning are used to support forms of credential acquisition (as well as practical knowledge building). Selwin understands you need to "teach them to first set out a plan, a five year development plan." Yvonne appreciates tacit knowledge as lifelong learning "you have to keep learning, be ahead...you always have to be learning." Nii identifies with "you have to know a lot about the functioning of education, the organization and the stakeholders you interact with."

All four forms of learning, formal, informal, non-formal and tacit learning all played an integral role in the educational development of current and future school leaders in Ghana, though it was the formal and non-formal that were recorded and which could be accumulated to support career mobility directly. Ironcially (given she is an educational leader) Nii partially debunks formal learning within the human capital theory by acknowledging that a degree does not mean that you can be an effective school leader; it simply can be interpreted that you have the academic discipline to achieve a goal. However, I believe a degree has many transferable skills of school leadership including written and verbal communication skills, building relationships and working in professional learning teams, etc. Non-formal learning in terms of additional qualification courses and general or specialist courses in education enhance one's portfolio. However, unfortunately the severity of financial limitations to many aspiring Ghanaians makes higher education unattainable even to initialize the first process of becoming a teacher.

SOCIAL CAPITAL

Canadian Data

The role of social capital in Canadian interviews was both overt and covert. In many cases, I felt like I had to read between the lines. Paul stated "at the school board level, you do need to know the levers of the school board because if you know different people at the board who can help you to access elements then that really does make a better school board." Sean believes

> ...it's not only who you know but who you know is helpful... it's someone you're having a coffee with and talking about the Leafs game – and you're talking about whatever else because these are your peers. These are your buds and it's absolutely critical in being an elementary school principal because you're alone and isolated." Edmund thinks "the key characteristic is the ability to build relationships."

Marina confesses I believe "the best principals are the ones that have an ability to get along with people." Vivian understands that:

> when you first walk into a school as a principal-no one knows you and your first task is to gain the credibility of those that you work with and those in the community and the only way that people will see whether you are credible or not is by what you do-talk is cheap and will only take you so far. People respect you for what you do-for what you accomplish, for what you stand for. Every decision made is communicating to the people around us who we are and I think that in order to gain respect and not necessarily admiration but respect of the people around you-you have to be the real deal.

Jasmind asserts "you need to have your finger on the pulse of what's happening in your community...working collaboratively." The focus on building networks in formal and causal settings is of note but the form is like an ameba constantly changing, growing and developing and you are not sure what shape or direction the relationship will go. Tony has a particularly warm approach,

> I've always seen the organization as a family and although we are huge within the confines of individual schools or a family of schools. There is a certain culture that is developed. Just like any family that matures, this is where you get your source of stability

and your source of safeness, we all have an input on how it is developed.

In sum, drawing on the data we can see that on the school board level, building networks can gain access to many specialized board-level personnel in various departments and aspects of the job. This is one level. The next level at school, it seems imperative to gain credibility amongst your school community in a respect-based collaborative environment. The family of schools is a good bridge between the school board networks and the school community. To expand upon the concept of networks in social capital, it encompasses influential mentors, supportive professional coaches and collegial, committee networks, etc. What begins to also become very clear here is that, beyond the description of social networks, we are building our social capital. Recapitulating Sean's believes "it's not only who you know but who you know is helpful…it's someone you're having coffee with and talking about the Leafs game – and you're talking about whatever else because these are your peers. These are your buds and it's absolutely critical in being an elementary school principal." There is the underlying requirement for specific forms of cultural knowledge necessary to do this; cultural knowledge that is enmeshed within hierarchies of race as well as gender. Just take this example: Who is it, we might ask, who typically has a familiarity with Toronto Maple Leafs hockey exactly? Is having coffee and discussing hockey part of the multicultural, plural or national professional norm within all organization? This is culturally specific within informal networks of privilege or some male gendered circles. However, there may be exceptions of visible minorities and women who would be invited into discourses and social settings such as these, yet, comfort levels and cross-cultural assimilations may come into play.

Ghanaian Data

Asenso declares "our school system here in Ghana is community-based." This is the premise of the Ghanaian education system. In these terms, social capital plays a large role in mobilizing group resources to create positive outcomes in schools. Elaine and Angelina echo the teamwork point within schools as well as explain how imperative it is to be involved in community activities. Jennifer discusses some of these teams: "the School Management Committee and the Parent Teacher Association meet and think about the school and how best the school will go." Integrity and duty are social capital qualities, Emmanuel brings up and extends his thought by saying that I "[try] to have good working relationships with my subordinates and let them feel they are a part of the system. You should be able to mobilize, work freely with other teachers. Have very good working relationships with other teachers to show that you can command respect and win their support by taking part in everything the community does."

Community stakeholders have a prominent role in education; however, Rose and Yvonne believe in having "good relationships with staff" as well. Kwame sees the principal as a parent; "you are the father for your teachers." Bettina says something similar in her interview. She says "you have to know human relationships, and how to deal with individuals...you have to know how to keep secrets as a head mistress of a school." Discretion and trust are important to building relationships necessary for functioning social networks. Developing this ability is expressed in terms of growing social capital. An aspiring educator or principal can feel isolated at times, but the notion that school leadership is an individual journey does not seem to apply to the case in this data from Ghana.

Despite the emphasis on credentials and objective ranking systems as well as my brief discussion of favouritism and barriers based on social class discussed earlier, here we see *that the community and staff appear to believe that they climb the ranks only with the support of others, as an imagery linking chain of hands clasped together and each school educator or administrator is at a different levels helping each other up.* Emmanuel discusses the benefits of informal networks, for example, "there were some students I taught when I was in teacher training college, who are now heads and we have an association of heads of basic schools in the municipality. We meet regularly to exchange ideas, share problems and make work smooth." But life cannot always work as smoothly as the linking human chain climbing and progressing together, Nala says "rather than put more injuries into their wounds, the problems at school...you have to co-operate to see their problem through." She acknowledges that there are problems like any professional community. Nii believes respect can combat this. Nii states "you need to first respect yourself, respect the people you are working with and the work...I go for discussions and suggestions to do my job...sometimes there are conflicts but we agree to disagree for better resolution."

My analysis suggests that the other foundational element to the Ghanaian education system other than human capital is social capital. They are part of each step of the career progression system. There is a strong discourse amongst Ghanaian administrators about the importance of supporting and helping each other along their career journey. Focusing on the tenets of trust, respect, duty, integrity and positive relations, informal networks and community-based modus operandi is central to the Ghanaian career promotional process and their education system as a whole. I agree with Nii who acknowledges that tension and conflict arises within every institution including schools because you are working with people. Having a positive and respectful attitude towards one another is essential not utopian, or unrealistic. This points to a social-emotional skill development process that needs to be a conscious daily practice.

CULTURAL CAPITAL

Canadian Data

Pierre Bourdieu helped us to realize that cultural capital is a system of social reproduction that exists in every form of organization and acknowledges that social differences are hierarchically organized. Examining cultural capital in an education context, we look at employee diversity and culture, occupational culture including school board and schools, language and power, values and (dis)positions. Dwayne looks to forecast the future climate of career mobility prospects for the coming years. He states:

> I think it was in terms of numbers and we're on the cusp of a lot of individuals retiring. A lot of our administrators are aging and the movement is a lot higher but you know what, this is all cyclical and this is going to end soon and it's going to become extremely difficult and very short lived. However, when the door of opportunity opens and one is not prepared, the window is only opened for so long...we have to go back to the universities. There's no way in which you can get a more diverse administrative group until you have a more diverse teaching group until you get some of those kids [that are] diverse looking differently to be in the universities because our profession is going to change tomorrow. We need to have our [visible minority] people with university degrees who can get into positions to become educators who can move to administration... we need to get those kids in the classroom so they see this as attainable.

Dwayne's statement touches the essence. The purpose of this study to inspire and assist marginalized groups including visible minority students and girls to aspire to be educators and later, school administrators. If there are no role models for them, it will not seem like a tangible reality for them.

The elementary, secondary and tertiary education systems as well as the school boards have a responsibility to be aware of the barriers that currently exist for visible minority students and girls in order, to overcome them so, they have a bright future to succeed in educational leadership for many generations to come. As Dwayne's comments help direct our attention forward; there may be a crucial window of opportunity.

The philosophy within some minority homes like Edmund's is:

I was the first born here and my [Chinese] parents would always tell me you need to work harder than people born here and were here for generations. I believe that but at the same time I think that when it comes to the actual selection of people it is based on the merit in front of the interview team reading the applications...I think a large part is what you have achieved and how people perceive that.

Merit needs to be coupled with access, Vivian believes:

I find that a real issue [for visible minorities] in saying to people-you know that there is a language of power and you need to be able to speak that language to gain admittance to the club...if you are looking to advance-you have to be prepared to use the language of power and to know how to give the appearance of someone who is educated and in the power position...you have to know how to look like them.

The *language of power*, assumes both being conscious of having to work harder than generations before and merit as having a key place within promotion; however, Bourdieu reminds us that we are not all playing on the same level field. The field has built in mechanisms of bias and privilege for the *community of power*. I agree with Vivian that the use of your education, understanding the vocabulary, articulations and power phrases and savvy within the *language of power* can help you to gain admittance in the *community of power* club. You may not receive full access but an entry point is somewhere to work from with acceptance from your power players of your organization. The *language of power* is a social construction of the dominant group, to recognize social difference it is important to encourage a *cultural language of power* that integrates into the dominant group's language of power to begin as an entry into systemic agency. The language of power means that there is a social cost for one's identity or asserting it. The cultural language of power is to be inclusive, representative of difference in the community one serves. I agree that merit is important, objective but the process and journey of career attainment has many subjective elements. Based on the comments coming from the data, I believe visible minorities stand to gain many insights and words of wisdom from oral tradition career stories and navigational insights from the past generations. At the same time, it is necessary to be critical of these forms of cultural knowledge and *language of power* to avoid simply reproducing forms of tokenism which in the end would only sustain inequitable career progression overall.

Vivian recognizes both the lack of racial and gender representation, but finds agency in the *language of power* to gain access in power circles in the school board. These power circles or power shakers demand a particular cultural presentation of one's self that is typically biased toward the make-up of the circle itself. Sean describes his perspective on this when he states:

> I think what is considered is how you carry yourself – how you speak- in order to be a good administrator. It's helpful if you're at least comfortable with people who are middle income or above because those are the people with power in this society...and if you can't deal with parents who have a bit of savvy and a bit of clout then, you're going to have some difficulty. The upper class, those are the power shakers here and they can make life miserable for an administrator if you're uncomfortable dealing with them. My family background is blue collar but having gone through college and university, it wouldn't be a huge impediment but it would be an impediment to career advancement certainly beyond principal to be a superintendent.

The *glass ceiling* in gender can be seen in terms of social class for someone like Sean. He has university education but feels his blue-collar upbringing puts a ceiling on his career advancement to the next level. My point is that Sean points to the forms of political savvy or cultural capital that is needed to maneuver in difficult situations which can relate to class, but race and gender as well. I too believe that it is important to understand power structures: know who runs them and it would seem that according to the data there is power in becoming comfortable with those who have power in the school board and school communities. Of course, for equitable changes this must work both ways. The *power shakers* at the top should know how to communicate with all class levels as well as all forms of social difference. Thus, there are some common threads of bias across race, gender and class. Understanding this within the career progression process may be a learned agency attribute.

Ghanaian Data

Cultural capital appears differently in Ghana. The racial tensions are ethnic based and the acknowledgements of such problems are sometimes associated with polarized opinions and sentiments. The attitudes on the *community of power* can have a variety of effects on the minority ethnicities. Emmanuel believes that because he is in the minority ethnicity, the Ga ethnicity, and he has attained his principal rank, that all other Ga can do it too. He says "how can a Ga become head of this school here then, if there is racial bias." This is not unlike the contradictions seen with the deaf principal in the Canadian data who has conflated different forms of social differentiation with each other and has deducted logical fallacies that because he has achieved an administrative position, he assumes there can be no systemic biases. Perhaps, I speculate that this Canadian principal, Oliver, conflated different forms of social differentiation due to protecting gender and his *community of power* and privilege, survival mechanisms, denial of asynchronic power relations and discrimination in the system, etc. But Selwin, a Ga principal has experienced *being downgraded*.

I believe that Emmanuel's argument is a little binary or *cut and dry*. There are many factors of promotion that need to be discussed such as minority ethnicities and other identity attributes, gender and age; lived experience with support systems in place or felt discrimination on their career journey. In explaining how he was downgraded by the *community of power* or the *dominant group*, in fact Selwin was cautious because of fear of consequence within his community that he may have acquiesced to privilege. In all professional organizations, Kwame believes there is *power in your language* like Canadian Vivian believes in a *language of power*. This knowledge helps produce personal agency and professional power within the currencies of competence in school leadership.

From currencies of competence to occupational culture, hiring processes suggest two major concerns. The first is the agency or lack of it for minority ethnicities. The divergent opinions with the minority ethnicities cause divisiveness in representation to mobilize for the educators coming up for promotion and the need for relationship bridging to form allies with the dominant ethnicity, intra-network and inter-networking within minority and dominant ethnicities. This runs in contrast to the broader discourse of helping others up the career ladder with linked hands as discussed earlier. There needs to be a fearless environment where minority ethnicities can voice their concerns. At the same time, within each ethnicity, people come from various socio-economic backgrounds, thus they do not compete on a level *'promotion' playing field*. Agency in this situation for aspiring educators could be to mobilize financial resources as a collective or bring the equity discrepancy in hiring practice as a collective.

Integration of Interactive Capital Data in the Mobility Field

In Canada, career mobility relates to knowing all the school community stakeholders. Approach the interview preparation process like a strategic marathon by reviewing current policies/practices, school board mission statements, consult retired and current principals that you respect, learn from good and poor examples of school leaders. Horizontal mobility has some merit such as resource positions. It is important to gain experience in different schools, grade levels, geographical locations and demographic backgrounds. Look for the future climate of career mobility to inspire and help the present students/children aspire to be school principals for the next generation.

Amongst the Canadian respondents, there were various terms associated with leadership such as sustainable, transformational, professional learning communities and leadership by demonstration. From the observation of individual leadership traits, the school community and school board can take a holistic look at leadership and how it is usefully exercised or not. The qualitative attributes were international experience, seniority, mentorship, high visibility assignments, political astuteness, innovation and creativity added to your organization and personality. This clearly surfaced in the Canadian interviews.

Just like identity is complex in terms of multiculturalism, pluralism, anti-racism so is the position of race in school promotion specifically. Some of the stances taken by respondents were: race as neutral, discrepancy regarding human rights, if one area of social difference is not discriminated against then it does not mean discrimination does not exist. There was reflection on race representation and the lack of visible minorities with school administration and the impact that it is having on the futures of our visible minority students. There have been some advances such as progressive surveys, employment equity policies, affirmative action but generations before still believe you have to work twice as hard to compete as a visible minority. Gender, power and politics play an important role within the school boards. In Canada, the old boys' network is alive and well. Historically, principal positions were only open for men. Percentages of inequality on the elementary panel were palpable. The promotion-family dilemma is apparent. Maternity leave keeps principal mothers out of the loop but it does sustain the school board's function as a whole by having children to sustain the institution. All of that aside, the Ontario Ministry of Education instituted a Leadership Development Initiative and Principal Mentorship program that assists mentors to support mentees to thrive in their Vice Principal and Principal roles as well as succeed in their family-work balance.

In terms of human capital in Canada, there are growing levels of educated professionals that are investing in higher education. They are attaining higher qualifications. Credentialism is of prime importance but access is a little easier due to available grants or loans. Social capital can exist as having informal networks with people who want to help you and support their initiatives. Socialize and find mutual interest and likeminded associates! Both social and cultural capitals were at play. In all cases, forms of inequity were possible to trace.

In Ghana, it appeared that horizontal mobility had relatively little value due to the strong orientation to the thirteen step ranking career progression system called "Placement of Teaching Staff". The problems in career mobility are in part related to the fact that there are no vacancies, many people wait for their current head master or mistress to retire and that could take 5 to 10 years. There are incentives in rural areas, younger candidates tend to sacrifice and move to these remote areas.

For the Ghanaian respondents, the term work hard arose for every interviewer but had various meanings such as implementing school change, staying current and continually learn, have good relationships, be able to manage school administration, be useful in community, be competent, fair and firm, etc. The quantifiable attributes were the dominant characteristics that emerged. They included superior job performance, good relationship with management and higher education. The overlapping themes with Canadian respondents were seniority and political astuteness worries of favouritism in promotion over family lines, neighbours, ethnic influence or same area affiliations.

In Ghana, racial issues manifests themselves in ethnic nepotism, and some respondents spoke of how during their job interviews bias appeared. Gender equity in Ghana appears to be thriving. Women have made great strides in school leadership. However, opposing views leave feminists and anti-feminist respondents at odds and the gender equity issue is bubbling underneath the surface in schools. Teacher replacements for maternity are becoming a serious problem and will continue due to the cultural significance of childrearing in a marriage and the duty to the husband's family.

Human capital is the predominant capital mobilized in the pursuit of upward mobility to school principal. The Ghanaian education system also depends on social capital. It is important to have good working relationships. It seems as though the unequal playing field of cultural capital is shaped by affluent families and unequal access to cultural knowledge.

Chapter 5

Changing the Direction of the Flow

Generating new directions in career theory...to re-establish the importance of this shared view of the career concept and to examine the process by which disciplinary cross-fertilization may help move [one's] career [forward].

(Arthur, Hall & Lawrence, 1989)

The purpose of this chapter is to synthesize the different factors affecting career mobility in interaction with one another. It will provide a more focused comparison between Ghanaian and Canadian respondents in terms of: career mobility, school leadership and politics within the organization; social difference factors of race and gender as well as building on the analysis of the interactions between human, social and cultural capital.

I would like to use the triangular models, tables and figure charts as visuals to reveal contradicting as well as overlapping themes that developed in the study for both Canada and Ghana. There are multiplicities of barriers within the career progression process. They are linked to political, cultural, financial and systemic/organizational factors. How these converge and diverge to paint a picture for an educator who is trying to gain access, enter and maintain a position of school leadership within a school board is essential. The historical references by the respondents of the limited access and equity for both visible minorities and women are palpable. Furthermore, the low representation of visible minorities and women on the elementary school leadership panel in Ontario and minority ethnicities in Koforidua gives currency to why this study is so necessary.

As educators, our primary purpose is the successful learning opportunities for our students. Our students need to see role models, representation and success within education and individuals within their community and gender flourishing as a school leader.

> What are the implications for these visible minority students? What are the voices of those visible minority educators and women who were successful and unsuccessful at times in their pursuit? What hardships and triumphs can they teach us? How can agency attributes assist those currently trying to aspire up the education ladder?

If we can visualize this in motion, the education ladder survives and thrives so that the few visible minorities and women school principals who came before would mentor the ones' struggling to figure out the system. Additionally, the ones who are trying to gain access currently are re-affirmed, supported and are successful in order, for the students of today to understand the importance of the support network within the pursuit of principal promotion. This chapter is informed by the following questions:

1. To what extent do the multiciplicity of career barriers play a role in the evidence of social differences and mobility?
2. How do the emerging themes from the data and the major research findings implicate the empowerment of marginalized individuals or groups in the education system?
3. How does the creation of the *Conscious Career Elevation* model advance the field of sociology, organizational development and career mobility? What further research implications does this study have on Canada, Ghana and other nations?

In order to address these questions, this chapter is organized as follows:
I. Synthesis of Multiple Factors in Interaction
II. Conscious Career Elevation
III. Integration of the Conscious Career Elevation Model

Synthesis of Multiple Factors in Interaction

Career Mobility and Education Leadership

Career mobility and school leadership respondents from both Canada and Ghana did formal preparation in terms of required academic qualifications filtered through school board (and state) regulations and policies. They also engaged in informal preparation such as interview preparation, staying current within the education field, and engaged in additional non-formal activities such as extra training sessions available to become better informed about the roles and responsibilities of the position. The central distinctions between the two countries' responses were political, cultural and financial in nature. In Ghana, as we saw in the previous chapter, the horizontal mobility seems to have little value. There are fewer vacancies. This creates a cause-effect or supply-demand issue. The gap implies that there are too many educators qualified for limited positions excluding rural schools' which requires great sacrifices. This causes a long retirement waiting period for aspiring educators of five to ten years of one's career, financial constraints of some educators to attend credentialed institutions, upper-echelon politics of family lines paying for promotions or ethnic nepotism. In Canada, networks and community connection, guidance and support of one's principal and superintendent or lack of it, timing of the availability in the education system of jobs, and career debates of horizontal mobility do seem to be valued as a viable experience. In addition, the generalist or specialist educator stance has contradicting values and pathways within one's career journey. This contradiction moves us from value shifts to orientations in career mobility.

To synthesize the overall orientations of respondents across the three career models of the ladder, spiral and web, I have tabulated results from the data in a bar graph. The figure below demonstrates which respondents were oriented to which career model. There are 17 respondents in both Ghana and Canada who oriented to the concept of the ladder, viewing career as a step-by-step progression. It weighed heavily on the Ghanaian side due to the systemic policy of "Placement of Teaching Staff" ranking system. There were two combinations of the ladder, the *spiral-ladder* created by three separate Canadian respondents who addressed it as swift moves with well-defined steps and the *web-ladder* invented by two Ghanaian respondents expressed gratitude to those who helped them initiate their first steps to attain the teaching job to then, begin climbing the ranks of their system.

Orientation to Career Models across Countries

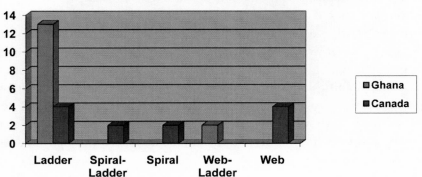

There were no Ghanaian respondents who chose the spiral while the two Canadian respondents related with the spiral as their career seemed to take a leisurely pace based on interest. Lastly, five Canadian respondents selected the web because the interconnectedness and relationships formed along the way.

In Canada, across the respondents there was significant evidence of the fostering of leadership through learning from strong, respected leaders. There was evidence of the valuing of empowering staff to exercise leadership in school, and the development of understanding the significance of the language of power and the potency it holds for attaining and sustaining positions of school leadership. Canadian respondents also spoke of learning from poor examples, building constructive relationships with school board personnel, colleagues and the school community enhances visibility and your professional learning network. In Ghana, most oriented to being able to set good examples in leadership, handle all your administrative affairs, have respect, integrity and good relations with school staff. The common thread between both countries was having respect for good leadership and learning from them. Other related threads were the language of power and transforming all relationships in the school to a positive and productive one. Despite the undesired qualities of leadership and honouring the good, ten agency attributes emerged from the study.

The *ten career agency attributes* which I discussed earlier in the study showed some consistencies and contradictions from the data in the interviews and the information taken from the survey-style questions as well. The interview data among the Canadian respondents revealed international experience, seniority, mentorship, high visibility assignments, political astuteness, innovation and creativity added to your organization and personality was valued. However, these respondents did not discuss higher education and superior job performance to a large extent. The reason why they did not discuss these attributes is critical to decipher. It is possible that education and superior performance was assumed as implicit. In other words, you could not even attempt promotion in school leadership if you did not have the required qualifications and high written evaluations. This could reflect Ontario having less structured institutional progression protocol. *Lock-step* structure or the ladder is the driving force behind the interviews from the Ghanaian respondents. The thirteen step structured format to be followed through a Ghanaian educator's career. The ranking structure, expectation and job function is explicitly stated for an educator to move forward in their career. The main expectation being that you compile your experience and model with excellence each step. There is both value and inequities to be found in both. Having a pre-determined career path has a finite plan and goal succession strategy in Ghana; however, an aspiring educator may not be able to pre-determine unforeseen barriers already in the system or the one's that might arise. In Canada, there are a variety of career pathways one could embark on and work towards yet it may not be a straightforward or a predictable path. Acknowledging this is overcoming one hurdle already.

Taking this into account, respondents were asked to rank ten career agency attributes through the use of my survey-style questions administered prior to the interviews, and these issues were discussed in the interviews.

To review, the ten career agency attributes that I traced in my earlier analysis of the data are as follows:

(1) Higher Education
(2) Superior Job Performance
(3) Personal Style
(4) High Visibility Assignments
(5) Influential Mentors
(6) Political Astuteness
(7) Seniority/Experience
(8) Good Relationship with Management
(9) Creativity/Innovation Added
(10) International Experience

Higher education (human capital) is a quantifiable measure. In both countries, there are certain educational requirements that must be met to become an educator as well as attain certifications, or additional degree programs to become a principal or seek an alternative promotion. There are varying degrees obtained to assist in management or alternate promotion such as Bachelor and/or Master of Education, Arts or Business, Doctorate in Education or Philosophy, Juris Doctorate or Post-Doctorate. Consequently, if you are aspiring to attain a position that requires a Master of Education, being in the position and taking into consideration the dynamics of race and gender within the attainment process, you feel the systemic pressure of trying to go beyond the minimum expectation. The competition becomes steeper and the feelings that respondents expressed regarding the need to do an extra degree or certification to enhance their qualifications was clear.

Superior job performance also has distinct characteristics such as dedication (requires after hours work), accuracy on daily tasks, punctuality, consistency or extra-curricular activities. Timing, achievement and effort all contribute to merit-based job performance. However, looking through a lens of a visible minority woman, superior job performance means "superior, superior" job performance. Women expressed this double effort in the interviews, she must be twice as good to be recognized or acknowledged. Superior job performance is partially rooted in human capital yet the over-compensation that visible minorities and women engaged in sheds light on the cultural capital dynamics at play on an unequal professional playing field.

Personal style is a qualitative attribute. It speaks to Ronald Heifeitz's perspective of leadership, self vs. role. (Heifeitz, 1994) *Self* interpreted as an individual's intrinsic qualities such as honesty, integrity, determination, etc. The *role* is as the external measure of a person or society's view. The issue of personal style suggests cultural capital was important. However, beyond Heifeitz, there were also the issues of identity related to racism, sexism and classism. Your personality or personal style that is exhibited daily influences co-workers and informs your colleagues who you are in adversity and success. Your "self" and your "role" are constantly competing in the spotlight of perception.

Seeking high visibility assignments speak to issues of human, social and cultural capital. Successful strategizing across these three forms of capital accumulation led to career mobility. Competence must be shown to larger numbers of influential members of your organization. This requires the building and application of cultural capital, but in a critical way so as not to lose one's own identity; it requires entry into social networks through which high visibility assignments can be garnered; and in part it depends on one's human capital since qualifications support being assigned important tasks. To emphasize the point, cultural and social capitals are linked to access and equity. Who is made aware of high profile assignments? In the often informal selection process, are the criteria in each assignment dependent upon an individual ability?

Obtaining *influential mentors* seems to depend on a combination of social and cultural capital accumulation. A mentor would help with career navigation and assist in terms of structure and knowledge with one's advancement. Does one's mentor have influence? Through the lens of identity, what is the likelihood of cross-cultural or gender mentor pairing? How many examples are there of an older male in the dominant racial group, in a position of authority mentoring a young visible minority woman? Is the answer that the transcending of roles can occur, unifying the mentorship process across difference? Or is this notion an unattainable goal? The data offered only anecdotes, sometimes second-hand stories, or simply expressions of empathy that allude to such cross-cultural supports. One of the contributing factors in the lack of examples revolve around the limitations in the development of broader forms of cultural capital (for both those in authority and those aspiring educators hoping to be mentored) expressed through expansive, cross-cultural social networking.

Regarding the notion of *political astuteness* – another example of cultural and social capital phenomena, I ask, does one have to have a strategy for career advancement? While, planning as well as setting a timeline for one's personal goals are crucial, another critical observation is the presence of an informal network. The informal network has influence on decision-making powers in your organization. A historical example is the concept of the *old boys' network*, a group of privileged men who dominate an organization. This type of informal network is exclusionary because certain people are accepted and are honored with access. Others within the same organization may not know that the network is presently operating and has pertinent information that could assist in one's career. However, reflecting on the data in both countries, gaining an invitation to such groups seems to suggest the need for specific forms of cultural knowledge or cultural capital which is unequally distributed across all marginalized groups including gender and race, and perhaps class as well.

School systems draw on credential attainment, merit-based, performance-based and *seniority*-based measures. This relates directly to human capital. In both Ghana and Canada, there are formal protocols that relate to merit, credentialization and performance. Some organizations have a monetary or acknowledgement reward system to reinforce power of seniority. Does an individual have to obtain a certain amount or number of years of experience to advance in an organization? In the Canadian data especially, we saw that seniority is not simply years of employment. Thus, another factor to consider is cross-functional job rotation or job specialization. Does the experience of job rotation assist in one's advancement? Does upward mobility require one to be recognized as the "expert" in one area, requiring diverse and specialized skill sets? The data reveals important barriers with regards to each of these questions.

Good relationship with management is a complex social and cultural capital issue, because it is dealing with value systems. There are many factors considered when thinking about maintaining a good relation with one's superior. Some attributes or values are integrity, initiative, effective listening and open communication, good conflict resolution skills, accountability, work stamina, encouragement and team building. The data shows collegial relations with your superior, collaborative efforts and beginning with your common denominator student learning and exercising leadership can improve your value added to your school.

Creativity and innovations added to your organization is a criterion that speaks to the mission and value of the organization. Looking at the data we see that individuals who consistently create ideas that impact the core objectives of the organization are usually recognized. Having an innovation that is perceived as worthy of distribution is important for growth. Innovations could be structural, personal or creative contributions that fundamentally change the functionality and essence of your organization. However, the opportunity to implement innovations is again rooted in accumulated forms of capital which is subject to uneven forms of access.

The last attribute, *international experience* can be interpreted through the lens of cultural capital. International experience across both counties was more or less valued due to the fact that it is based on exposure. Exposure clarifies the understanding of the education system in a broader cross-cultural context and the cultural capital accumulated through the learning that takes place in global teaching environments can support advancement. What kind of global experience is most valued? In the data, some educators explored these avenues through vacations, summer work abroad, living/working abroad, student exchanges, international conferences and/or teacher exchanges. Consequently, the class and fiscal capital factor limits access or deny some educator's of these experiences.

Now having synthesized the findings from earlier in relation to the ten career agency attributes based on the interview data, we can now turn to the results of respondents' ranking of these attributes themselves for further cross-national observations. In the table below, the ranking results of respondents in each country were averaged. The results represent the ranking by respondents from each country that indicated the importance of a specific attribute for effective career agency: a higher number represented less importance (e.g. a ranking of 10th in importance) and lower number represented the most importance ascribed to an attribute (e.g. ranked number one). Respondents were encouraged to select number rank per attribute as they felt appropriate to their experience. The survey-styled questions data or ranking results are seen on the chart below:

Results of the Ten Career Agency Attributes for Ghana and Canada

TEN ATTRIBUTES	RANK OF ATTRIBUTE IN KOFORIDUA, GHANA	RANK OF ATTRIBUTE IN TORONTO, CANADA
Higher Education Attainment	1	2
Superior Job Performance	2	1
Personal Style	7	4
High Visibility Assignments	6	8
Influential Mentors	8	6
Political Astuteness	10	9
Seniority/Experience	4	3
Good Relationship With Management	3	7
Creative and Innovation Added to Your Organization	5	5
International Experience	9	10

The ranking results yielded basic trends that mostly, though not always, matched the findings from the interview with both Ghanaian and Canadian respondents. In Ghana and in Canada, the two quantifiable attributes were interchangeable as primary and secondary in importance: higher education and superior job performance. This is consistent with what the respondents stated in their interview. In Ghana, human capital, credentials and qualifications are of highest importance. In Ontario, you simply cannot apply without a Bachelor's degree and two specialists or a Master's degree and the Ontario Ministry of Education requires you to have your Principal Qualification Program, Part I and II. In addition, you need an exemplary performance appraisal and written recommendation from both the principal and superintendent. This holds a lot of credence in the application process, placed in the educator's employment file within organization and strongly influenced their career journey. The value of these attributes is not simply accorded within the local organization, but is often a shared standard across regions and countries. Higher education and superior job performance are two career agency attributes that seem to present themselves as universal career principles.

There was an important discrepancy between the information shared in the interviews and the recorded ranking about the career agency attribute of political astuteness. Both the Ghanaian and Canadian respondents discussed testimonials, insights and observations about political astuteness. These discussions related to social networking and the issues of corruption, nepotism, exclusion or deliberate lack of support. However, both Ghanaian and Canadian ranked political astuteness as last or second to last. The political arena for the respondents was lived through spoken word and experience. There seems to be a disconnection between conscious awareness of the importance of this attribute and the descriptions of the need for political astuteness in the course of career progression.

In both Ghana and Canada, international experience was ranked either last or second last. Despite the value that most of the respondents ascribed to this attribute in their interview, it is possible that, due to financial barriers of many teachers such experiences were seen as a luxury.

The middle ranked career agency attribute for both Ghanaian and Canadian respondents was creativity and innovation added to your organization. I suspect that this is due to the balance of the kind of idea, ingenuity, innovation and benefit the project or idea would have to the organization. It is important to note, this attribute is in the middle, taking a democratic stance. This democratic stance tells the aspiring educator to proceed with caution giving ideas but also supporting existing ideas and current school administrators in their vision is also important. The implementation process of a new initiative or innovation at the school board or school level needs key supporters to assist in foreseeing barriers and helping to navigate them if they arise.

Seniority and experience were very close to the top in rank for both Ghanaian and Canadian respondents in the ranking data, but the meaning of this attribute is distinctive in the two countries. The interview mostly reinforced that broad forms of experience are necessary, though horizontal mobility in Ghana was not as highly valued generally speaking. At the same time, the interviews highlighted some of the struggles the Ghanaian respondents had with the experience differential between younger school administrators and seasoned educators in terms of respect for the young administrator – collaborative decision-making and shared power within inclusive leadership gave agency in these situations. The Canadian respondents addressed frustrations where an educator had narrow experience, for instance, spending twenty years in Grade 7. In Canada in particular, it seems that diversifying your experience has value.

In Ghana, maintaining a good relationship and selecting high visibility assignments are important parts of Ghanaian career mobility. Moreover, Ghana's education system appears strongly oriented toward human and social capital. The respect of the current principal's education and work ethic and being able to exemplify that you *work hard* within highly visible community programs is one of the indicators of success within promotion. In Canada, personal style and finding a mentor are rooted in social and cultural capital and connect to obtaining high visibility assignments. This highlights a combination of self-determining factors and learned traits, informal networks and the access to a mentor that will provide support in the career mobility process. These career agency attributes that varied in rank from three to eight were good relationship with management, high visibility assignments, personal style and influential mentors. In Ghana, by gaining the opportunity to receive a high visibility assignment at the school board or education unit is competitive and valued, and contributes to assisting your career. In Ontario, high visibility assignments, experience and promotion have other implications for outside organizations such as the teachers unions, education departments in colleges/universities and the ministry of education. Influential mentorship, aligning yourself with a person you respect that is in the role you aspire to is essential to the career mobility process in Canada, having someone to *show you the ropes,* the mechanisms, savvy and skill-performance levels needed for the position. Finally, the career agency attribute of having a good relationship with management also varied among the ranking data set of both Ghanaian and Canadian respondents. It is possible that this could be due to the differences in the way that community and the individual are emphasized in the Ghanaian and Ontarian social difference data in terms of race and gender in both Ghana and Canada.

Social Difference-Race and Gender

Race, ethnic or visible minority issues manifest themselves very differently in Ghana than in Canada. In particular, as we saw earlier, Ghana is a homogeneous society in terms of race; however, the diversification exists in ethnic origins. The minority ethnic head masters or mistresses spoke candidly about their ethnic frustrations within the school system, and many principals from the Ashanti ethnicity [dominant ethnicity] did not acknowledge discriminatory practices. Ewe and Ga ethnicities, the minority ethnicities found agency in their own ethnicity assembly or informal network of support. These minority ethnicities spoke about some strides made in formal or informal educational network groups that unite all ethnic groups and share knowledge and success tips of the school administration trade.

In Ontario, the school system serves one of the most diverse populations in the world and race for many years had been under scrutiny. The rising numbers of racial discrimination and human rights violations that are reported are at an all time high not to mention the ones that are not reported. Those school administrators in the dominant group or culture had opposing views: some were neutral to race, professed only school board equity while others' empathized with colleagues who are a visible minority and their journey. Race is so salient in Ontario yet it remains taboo, and when spoken of often falling on deaf ears. Visible minority educators wanted to speak out about racial or ethnic discrimination in their current reality but fear the consequence on their career or daily practice. This study addresses an educator's mobility and the empowerment tools for career navigation.

The table below gives a comparative summary of the survey-styled questions in the data set based on gender. The questions summarized in the table were: (1) does a male or female occupy the highest educational position in your nation or province, (2) what is the female to male ratio in school leadership representation, (3) which countries have support systems in place at work and at home for women on maternity, family-work balance, (4) are their inclusive or exclusive networks that males or females have such as old boys' network, gender nepotism and so on. The gender comparisons are very interesting due to the polarity in present power situations within the school board and government jurisdictions. For example, the first point on the table indicates that in Koforidua, Ghana the current General Director of Education is a woman and in Ontario, Canada, in 2006, the current Premier of Ontario and both school boards interviewed had male Directors of Education.

Gender Analyses for Ghana and Canada

GHANA	CANADA
• Female General Director • More female principals than males • Both male and female have feminists and anti-feminists views • Women have many children more valued in family-community structure than career • Maternity leave supply replacement problem, impediment for women's career • Current political climate supportive of women's promotion, men in minority in the elementary panel	• Male - Premier of Ontario and school board's Director of Education • Females acknowledge the old boys' network and males deny it. • Many women have family-work balance and others aspire to this • Maternity leave, payment and replacement met by policy • Current Political Climate, there is a significantly lower number of female principals on the elementary panel • Males have informal networks in social activities, male family nepotism or legacy exists

The survey-styled questions in the data set for Canadian respondents were consistent; however, many male respondents checked that they support females in their promotional endeavors but the gender representation tells us otherwise. One respondent wrote at the back of her sheet that it was twice as hard to gain access to a superintendent position as well as principal for women and visible minorities. The data for Ghanaian respondents do not indicate that there is a gender problem but there is a discrepancy: the interviews reveal the sting of men resenting a female General Director and its influence on the education system in Koforidua.

The polarization of views on power in gender relations is detectable. Ghanaian women are empowered by the access to key power position within the organization and are able to mobilize the female network and gain the respect of their colleagues by being a dominant force, support and awareness of gender issues in Ghana. There is also an understanding of how important it is to maintain this because if the power structure shifts all of the strides made by Ghanaian female educators could be 'derailed' as a Ghanaian respondent mentioned. There is key learning for Canadian female educators from the *power plays*, support networks amongst women and the mobilization gained by women within the Ghanaian education system. How did the Ghanaian female educators' minimize the effects of the *old boys' network* that existed for many years in Ghana? Clearly there were qualified female educators waiting in the wings for their opportunity. When that moment came, their academic and community savvy was there to capitalize on the opportunity. In terms of the maternity-family factor, in Canada career delay and inability to stay current of the issues within the school board can and do exist. In Ghana, Ghanaian female educators' have much to contend with in terms, of replacement issues and the frequency of maternity leave as a societal value lends to much accommodation with many needed resources to support this.

Human, Social and Cultural Capital

In Canada, concerning *human capital* and educational attainment the respondents attained their credentials/degrees, specialist courses, gaining skills through in-services and workshops as their human capital investment. The Ghanaian respondents were highly focused on human capital accumulation as each respondent discussed the formal learning (degrees and qualifications) and non-formal (additional qualification courses). As we saw, this was a strong element of career progression in the Ghana context.

Social capital had equal value by both Canadian and Ghanaian but in divergent ways. Social capital manifests itself for Canadian respondents in these central forms of social and professional interaction by having a family of schools or many schools in network, school board relations, parent-school relations and the community relations including tertiary education and the media. Social capital revealed itself for Ghanaian respondents as the schools were viewed as being community-based. Schools are not only a learning institution for children; they have functioned as crisis-centres, health assistance, food and clothing centres for the community. These social capital interactions, networks and community committees are vital for career mobility in both Ghana and Canada. Both countries realize that the key to advancement of your person and your profession is building relationships with your colleagues and the people in your community.

Cultural capital has taken on different forms in these two countries. In Canada, the respondents' spoke of not having an equal professional playing field in promotion in terms of race and gender representation, the use of the *language of power* to gain access and the importance of representation for the next generation of visible minority and female educators. In Ghana, the respondents' inequity focus was on minority ethnicity representation linked with socio-economic class limits of financial opportunity, inequity and possibly instances of corruption. In both countries, the lack of representation in minority racial/ethnic groups in school leadership has been a sustained problem. The forms of agency discussed were formalized professional networks among both minority and dominant groups to come together to gain the breath and depth of the problem. This suggests that in both Ghana and Canada, the *community of power* is divided. On one hand, the community of power in these formal networks purport that they want to assist to breakdown the hegemonic matrix of difference that exists in promotion, and on the other hand, the community of power does not want to lose their privilege within the organization.

The comparative synthesis of Ghanaian and Canadian data is organized against the backdrop of the mobility field (See Chapter 4).

Human, Social and Cultural Capital Diagram

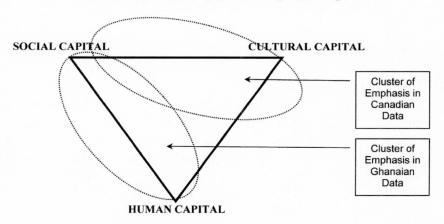

The following table attempts to show the different clusters of emphasis that respondents in Ghana and Canada spoke to across human, social and cultural capital accumulation processes. The light, dotted ovals signal where the majority of emphasis is placed in the two situations. Ghanaian responses tended to cluster around social and human capital processes, with less attention paid to cultural capital. In comparison, Canadian data suggested greater emphasis of social and cultural capital processes with less concern for human capital accumulation. At this point, it is important to recall the theoretical underpinnings of the mobility field such as career mobility as vertical or horizontal, the career ladder, spiral and web, educational leadership, power, privilege, positions and dispositions of social difference in terms of race and gender. These theories help us to understand the respondents' insights, knowledge and experience that are explored in the diagram below.

The orientation to social capital processes is shared across the two countries. The field of education involves the learning process of students, teachers, administrators and community alike. The professional networks, mentors, coaches and supportive roles emphasize social capital and point toward the importance of the career theory of the *web*. As we saw in the Orientation to Career Models across Countries, while the *ladder* is an orienting conceptual metaphor for both Ghanaian and Canadian respondents, an orientation to the web is the only other conceptual metaphor that is shared by both groups. Mobilizing group resources and building positive professional relationships are an important element of understanding both an education system and its promotional process. A related goal of analyzing these issues, however, is also to translate findings to practical tools for minority women educators in relation to conscious strategy in relation to career progression. In this regard, we can now turn toward a discussion of career elevation.

Conscious Career Elevation

Multiplicities of Career Barriers within School Leadership

The *Conscious Career Elevation (CCE) model* is meant to offer a summary of strategy for intentional career mobilization and navigation within systems of power for marginalized people. This term is based on acknowledging the possibility of personal agency within networks of domination, despite significant constraints and systemic inequities. As I noted from the beginning of this study, the ideological climate of educational systems reflect systems of hegemony and the resistance.

The essence of the Conscious Career Elevation model is to be aware of the ten attributes developed in this research along with matters of different forms of capital accumulation in order that marginalized groups both understand that they are in a complex, tension-filled, pressure cooker situation, and that there are specific means of navigation for dealing with this situation. This tension stems from the need to challenge the system. The mere acknowledgement that there are personal and professional inequities creates tension and disequilibrium.

The disequilibrium can create openings in the system to navigate and attain promotion. However, we need to understand that there is a fine line between consciousness and consequence in the system. Marginalized educators need to hone their competencies on a conscious social, political and intellectual level. Additionally, as levels of consciousness grow and educators have moments to exercise leadership by discussing social barriers that could be consequences which, for the purposes of this study, can sometimes result in what are often called a *career limiting move*. The tension speaks to the need to change the racial and gendered face of an educational system while not acquiescing and losing our identity.

The use of the Conscious Career Elevation model is meant to be a mechanism to produce choice for subordinate social groups, but it remains situational and not a one size fits all solution. One can extrapolate the effects of one or all ten attributes, as well as locate the problem and oneself on the mobility field. In many ways, the resiliency of one principal who took it upon herself to take the promotion process like a *strategic marathon* is embedded in this model. She was conscious of a great many of the mechanisms and barriers, and she planned with intention and purpose. This was purposeful and it is in line with the CCE model. I argue that taking a closer look at the ten attributes in the CCE model will deepen a sense of their usefulness for the various situations and scenarios that an individual could be faced with in dealing when dealing with the politics and "know-how" of promotion.

Conscious Career Elevation (CCE) Model

The Conscious Career Elevation model seen below incorporates many dimensions of analysis. In addition to the attributes, the mobility field is also part of the model's backdrop. This triangular field consists of human capital, social capital and cultural capital. This mobility field is fluid; it is meant to represent mediational relations between factors with human capital at the bottom and the social or cultural capital on either side. In other words, this field is shifting and situational as leadership opportunities and oppression intersects. It is up to the person who finds herself in any given instances of intersection to exercise choice and use whichever capital she has accumulated in a strategic manner understanding that there are embedded inequities in the system. One might choose to use human capital as a form of agency, relying on credentials, formal schooling and practice. Or, one might use social capital to mobilize people who are leaders in a school board. Or, one could draw on one's own cultural capital to support interactions with individuals or networks of people. As noted, it is absolutely crucial to recognize that these forms of capital, like the notion of power itself, are not neutral: race and gender inequities shape the accumulation of these different types of resources. Nevertheless, I argue that understanding these different resources including the means and barriers to accumulating them can help both the researcher and the educator to understand the power dynamic of the situation in order to come up with a creative solution to career mobility problems.

By laying out the foundation of the mobility field, we can now see how the Conscious Career Eleveation tools play out in the field. To recall, the ten attributes are:

- *(1) higher education,*
- *(2) superior job performance,*
- *(3) personal style,*
- *(4) high visibility assignments,*
- *(5) influential mentors,*
- *(6) political astuteness,*
- *(7) seniority/experience,*
- *8) good relationship with management,*
- *(9) creativity and innovations added to your organization,*
- *(10) international experience*

It is important to note that the central tenet that holds the CCE Model together is the concept of creating openings for change, in effect, strategically playing on the tensions between different forms of capital and different types of attributes within a hegemonic system.

Let's face it, as we engage in attaining higher levels of education, as we, the minoritized presence learn about being politically savvy and what personal style of leadership is successful; we, in turn, increase the tension surrounding our promotional potential. In addition, by using our consciousness of what being marginalized means within an organization, we owe it to ourselves to be extremely familiar with which organizational policies work in our favour, and those which do not. This legitimizes the tension and validates the need for change in the area of promotion. Are there consequences for this kind of action? Tipping the power scale of any organization may have consequences, such as social ostracization, subject to hurtful gossip, penalties in gaining opportunities, opposition with authority figures in the organization, etc. The point is that marginalized groups including the minoritized female professionals can become better equipped with policy, credentials, social savvy by drawing on awareness through the type of CCE model developed here.

The aim of the Conscious Career Elevation model was to provide a "how to" navigation tool to assist in career progression. Each marginalized person, the *tension* is within a different organization, contending with different politics and struggles to contend with when seeking promotion.

I respect the varied entry points of individuals and I want the Conscious Career Eleveation model to be seen as using the empowerment tools that are relevant to each marginalized person's situation with an understanding that they can be further empowered by their human, social and cultural capital in the face of inequality.

Conscious Career Elevation Model (CCE)

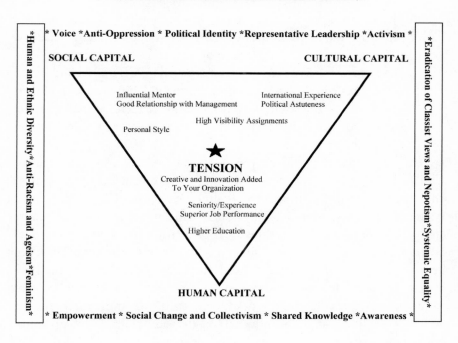

The Conscious Career Elevation model informs the research, but its' not limited to just this particular promotional scenario. This is how the CCE model contributes to the field of career and organization development:

(1) The individual is represented by the star at the centre of the model. This is also the point of tension in the sense that, ultimately, the tensions of the system are felt by individuals in their lives.

(2) From here the individual is presented with a series of organized choices: where to put her energies in terms of attributes and the relation of these attributes to different forms of capital accumulation.

(3) The model inherently expands the field of choice for aspiring teachers by offering a means of organizing their awareness of attributes and the development of different types of (human, social and cultural capital) resources.

(4) The various issues at stake in this navigational process are represented in the terms bordering the figure on the top, bottom and sides: issues of diversity, anti-racism, anti-classism, feminism and their counterparts such as favourtism, nepotism, corruption, etc.

(5) It is also important to note the two categories of career mobility that this model encompasses as expressed in the CCE table above. The first category, horizontal mobility, is the lateral progression in one's career. It is essential to note that the CCE Model and its ten attributes could be used in both horizontal and vertical mobility. Focusing on the latter, the tension seems to increase at a faster rate in vertical mobility possibly because of competition for limited positions.

As we saw in the previous chapter for example, Canadian interviewee Carol addresses this tension by stating "there are related implications to cultural, gender and class differences and have more of an impact when trying to attain a position above the school administration level." The more competitive or scarce the positions are, (for example the positions of school board superintendents or the Director) the narrower the space seems to be for individuals who represent social difference. This is exactly the kind of systemic problem that the Conscious Career Elevation model is meant to target. However, its efficacy depends both on the individual and her ability to mobilize, or have influence on decision-making powers in an organization, or create more spaces in the organization for breaking through tensions, leading to sustainable change. Change can be conceptualized on a continuum at both endpoints there is conflict and consensus, and the middle tension is the arena of change. The middle tension needs to be ripe in the education system and the philosophies of its stakeholders for sustainable change to happen. The CCE Model does relate to the international comparative dimension of the study in terms of both Ghana and Canada.

Integration of the Conscious Career Elevation Model

Examining different types of human, social and cultural accumulation and how it intersects with social difference will inform an educator's journey as she attempts to advance professionally. Can this pursuit be accomplished better with social, human or cultural capital? Can a minoritized educator navigate a successful track to promotion considering the embedded barriers in the system? How large is the role of social difference in including or excluding one who is being considered for promotion? This research of career mobility addresses this line of questioning. Hill-Collins (2000) referenced in previous chapters examine the hegemonic matrix of difference in relation to school leadership practices.

> "To maintain power, dominant groups create and maintain a popular system of "commonsense" ideas that support their right to rule. Hegemonic ideologies concerning race, class and gender are often so pervasive that it is difficult to conceptualize alternatives to them, let alone ways of resisting the social practices that they justify" (Hill-Collins, 2000).

Thus, the exclusionary hidden practices, dominate social networks, nepotism and social bias highlight the politics of social difference at stake here.

The ten agency attributes in the Conscious Career Elevation model are empowerment tools for individuals who face political inequities and find themselves unable to gain access to promotional opportunities in education administration. How can an elementary school administrator manage micropolitics successfully and lead inclusively, when school leaders and staff have differentiating value systems? It is important to find allies and encourage dialogue in scenarios such as this.

Inclusive leadership, Ryan (2005) envisions a democratic, emancipatory, participative, distributive, shared and teacher leadership exhibiting different degrees of inclusion.

These approaches include a culmination of education stakeholders such as education practitioners, parents, students to inform policy and school decision-making. Ryan's leadership approach, connecting critical-democratic practice, finding agency in allies, and liberatory participation has much merit, as long as systemic savvy is simultaneously exercised.

> I think it is also important for a policy to be reflective of the demographic and all of the constituents involved; it connects all educators and disadvantaged groups involvement. This kind of involvement makes equity a non-negotiable option and sets a precedent of importance.

This reinforces the sense of urgency felt when dealing with something like inclusiveness that affects all people within an organization, especially the marginalized ones. A deeper understanding and connection for an administrator to make is through examining the link between privileged educators and disadvantaged groups of students and staff. A school leader and educator can orient and adapt their experience to the life experience of their students. A valuable extension of this is to try to formulate constructive partnerships with school and community stakeholders to raise awareness about these connections and consider them in decision-making and policy changes.

The counter to inclusive leadership practices is the understanding that there are different types of exclusionary practices. What are the *hidden exclusionary practices* that are rampant in the education system or schools that are cleverly overlooked? Elements such as the school board culture or climate, principal initiatives or involvement, who is considered a qualified candidate, old informal network dominance, unidentified nepotism, being negatively politically labeled, etc. are all hidden exclusionary practices. Thus, there are structural changes that are needed to ensure equitable practices for promotional opportunities within one's school board.

Being politically cognizant of inclusive leadership and exclusionary practices, and practicing the ten agency attributes' for career mobility is how one provides a pathway for political agency with savvy and astuteness. A *career mobiliter* needs to construct a solid strategy for career advancement. The plan and execution of the implementation process, as well as setting a timeline for one's personal goals are crucial. The use of the ten agency attributes is an initializing process for each career step or position attained; and can also be used for *career maintenance* in new roles and responsibilities accrued.

Chapter 6

Moving the Flow Forward

Finding partners, adjusting the [career] thermostat, pacing the work, making your interventions unambiguous and timely, bringing attention back to the issue, and showing the relevant communities a different future than the ones they imagine...

(Heifeitz & Linsky, 2002)

This chapter summarizes the major research findings of the study. It shows the development of social difference, leadership and career mobility aspirations for elementary school practitioners in Ghana and Canada. By providing context for the data, it became necessary to take a critical lens when examining the findings and relate it back to the original research questions. In the previous data analysis and synthesis chapter, the analysis revealed patterns of prominence in success with certain attributes such as political astuteness and seniority. However, all ten attributes have merit in the context of mobilizing one's position of promotion within an organization. The Conscious Career Elevation (CCE) model is a strategy and career tool to give awareness and informs marginalized educators how to navigate an inequitable system. This chapter's goal is to inspire marginalized individuals or groups that have been disenfranchised by the education system. With this goal in mind, the discussion in this chapter is informed by the following objectives:

1. What are the researchers' reflections and what implications do the reflections and findings have to create systemic and individual reform?
2. Can marginalized groups capitalize on human, social and cultural resources in the education system?
3. How does the creation of the *Conscious Career Elevation* model assist in gaining personal resiliency and agency, finding allies in both privileged and disadvantaged groups to create systemic change?

In order to address these questions, this chapter is organized as follows:
I.   Overall Themes Emerging From the Data
II. Reflections on my Journey as the Researcher
III. Implications of the Study
IV. Flowing With the Stream

Overall Themes Emerging From the Data

In terms of career mobility, leadership and agency attributes, in survey-styled questions both Ghana and Ontario selected higher education and superior job performance; because that was the quantifiable or a tangible goal that is required for the position (such as a degree or a high performance evaluation). However, the survey-styled questions and the interviews showed contrasting results. Seniority and political astuteness were valued in both Canadian and Ghanaian interviews; and the results of the ranking survey-styled questions were political astuteness where the least highly ranked attributes for both Ghana and Canada. Political astuteness as a subject is either taboo or is seen as unfavorable conversation. If it was socially acceptable to openly recognize politics within one's organization, it would bring consciousness to the interactions at play in both Ghana and Canada. Yet the ideology of a straight-forward meritocracy is also alive and well. In effect, however, it is an ideology that consistently does not serve subordinate groups but rather resists the possibility of strategic action. For all marginalized groups including visible minorities and women, sustaining this ideology is inadequate. Rather I argue and attempt to demonstrate that they must strive to recognize the multiple dimensions of the Conscious Career Elevation model including activism, empowerment, voice, eradicating racism, gender-bias and nepotism. I would like to use politics, privilege and power, as the "3 Ps" because they are alive and well, yet many individuals continue to deny the three "P's" existence. However, the benefits of human, social and cultural professional informal networks benefits both aspiring educators and principals in Ghana and Canada.

The survey-style questions indicated some insights that differed from the in-depth interviews. The seniority/experience was recognized to be of importance, and a reward system was noted for having a certain amount of years of experience (rewards included such accolades as professional incentives, access to other positions, community recognition, etc). However, the "kind" of experience became important to note seen in the surveys of both Canadian and Ghanaian respondents. In Ghana, merit was accomplished evenly both to cross-functional job rotation and specializing. In Ontario, cross-functional job rotation seemed to be important, experience different grades, divisions, schools and demographics. Lastly, a good relationship with management varied in Ghana, but generally was perceived to be of high importance, and in Ontario, it is more mildly regarded, sometimes simply implicit in how interviewees understood their experiences. I postulate that the response on this issue in Ontario is due to union issues. Both Ghanaian and Ontarian principals thought "creativity and innovation added to the organization" has a standard role. New ideas are what distinguish organizations from one another. The other qualitative attributes were personal style, in which many respondents commented that it does in fact impact mobility potential. Regarding influential mentors, many principals took responsibility for their own career development; others think mentors, school board management and family is responsible for career development. The majority of the respondents had a strategy and implementation plan for their career development with a specific timeline. In addition, the majority do think that having a mentor within the school board to assist with career navigation is very helpful.

In terms of the three career mobility images of the ladder, the spiral or the web, the majority of respondents reported to have progressed in the fashion of the ladder, proceeding step-by-step in Ghana. The two that meandered created a web-ladder emphasizing the importance of the community in their beginning stages of teaching. In Canada, combinations of the spiral-ladder caused variation; the spiral was viewed as a pace-setting process of the step-by-step progression of the ladder such as stopping to have a family, medical leave, etc. The web was seen in terms of connection to people and networks that helped career progression; the idea of community recommending, assisting and supporting one's decisions, triumphs and failures and process of attainment.

The emerging social difference themes involving interrogating race and gender was enveloped in power and politics such as politics of representation, identity, intersectionality, community and the individual. Due to the nature of being a cross-cultural study, the shifting definition of minority changed within a Canadian context and Ghanaian context. To be a minority in Canada is to be a visible minority or racialized, seen as not in the dominant group. In Ghana, the minority group was represented by minority ethnicity such as Ewe or Ga; the dominant ethnicity was Ashanti-Twi. The representation of minority language groups among school principals was comparable to the racialized minorities in Canada among school principals. Yet linguistic and cultural differences are distinct from the visibility-power of racialization. The first, in principle, allows some opportunity for passing in a way that the second seems to resist more strongly. Politics of identity and intersectionality is vital to the orientation of this research such as being both a visible minority and a female. A goal was to see, when competing multi-oppressions faced an individual aspiring for leadership, what agency did she have left to exercise?

The politics of the individual is that personal agency is imperative, but without the support of the community on her journey for promotion, it becomes much more difficult. With negative essentializing of minority cultures, it is important to mobilize as a community. The reality is that internalized racism or identity does exist. Internalized racism or identity is changing and become more intense than in earlier times, and the consequent fracturing of the community is becoming more apparent. This widens the gap for community solidarity within organizations, such as denying one's identity, causing separation from one's community, self-defeating actions that take the responsibility away when it should be back in the hands of the individuals in the community. In other words, when interrogating marginalized groups including race and gender within its communities, it is important to note visible minorities and women need to mobilize the full range of their capitals: social, human and cultural. With respect to social capital: is there a presence of supportive networks and mentors? Turning to human capital: can visible minority or woman principals support aspiring educators in their school leadership applications, for example through written or verbal recommendations or mentorship? Finally, regarding cultural capital, can visible minority principals and women share their experiences in the education system with each other, thus increasing their collective access to information? There is a fine line between cooperation and competitiveness. Cooperation within the community is critical. Competitiveness should be directed at beating one's personal best in a strategic marathon of promotion. Misplaced competition amongst individuals and groups de-energizes the community and causes retrograde in the collective process. This is a core contradiction endemic to the promotional process: competitiveness is central by the nature of the process, yet for subordinate social groups cooperation is important as well.

For gender, I examined the glass ceiling, male escalator, old boys' network and historical male dominated promotional process now, leaving female educators to look for access to overcome barriers. Both the Ghanaian and Ontarian system operate according to a grid standard or rank system as an educator. Consequently, if fewer women are being promoted, and there is an invisible cap of promotability, the glass ceiling, it calls into question the field of education and the teacher-promotion gap for female elementary educators who are, in both countries, the majority. Specific to fields where there are high populations of female teacher employees, men have a fast track to promotion, the male escalator which seems to tip the equality scale. On the elementary school panels, there are visibly significant higher numbers of female teachers in the Ghanaian and Canadian education systems. However, when it comes to management or principal leadership, the positions are filled disproportionately by men. However, it is important to note that the disproportionate number of male educators to boys in the elementary system; this is also a gap that needs to be closed for all students to succeed.

The findings show that historically, men were groomed for these leadership positions. Historically and currently, men have been informally asked or got the tap on the shoulder, to be a part of the old boys' network, an informal group that shares information among men to ensure their promotional success in the least amount of time required. Keep in mind, a visible minority male may not have access to this form of privilege within an organization or his savvy may give him access. Due to the scarcity of males in this field, men have an escalator to the principal position. This is happening simultaneously while some women are competing for the positions, causing divisiveness between female teachers and unequal promotional practice. Other female educators and principals consciously look to give back from the dominant and minority groups and assist in career navigation advice.

We can see that human, social and cultural capital accumulation are all relevant factors that shape the odds of success at the starting line and throughout the career race. We use all of our energy to shape and cultivate ourselves, to hone these skills and execute them within our organization. Is it a question of which capital wins or is important that all forms of capital keep the pace and cross the finish line at some point? They all must cross the finish line to gain access to promotion, and at times they may have been overlapping one another on the track due to different rates of accumulation of the different forms of capital. But, all are needed in the development of a professional and a leader. A school principal needs all of those forms of capital, she also needs discipline to attain credentials, understand the complex social dynamics and networks in her environment, as well as have an awareness of the inequities and potential barriers that may exist. In Canada, with the backdrop of human capital, cultural capital comes to the foreground needing support from social capital networks. In Ghana, with the backdrop of cultural capital, human capital comes to the foreground also needing support to sustain oneself with community networks, social capital. I believe one of the most significant contributions stated by a respondent was the notion of having and using the language of power by the Canadian Vivian. The language of power gives access to marginalized individuals to gain respect and earn some accountability within their social circles.

Reflections on my Journey as the Researcher

As the researcher, I began the project feeling that "I may be sitting down but I am standing up inside." Now, I feel that sentiment even stronger. I understand that there could be "blind spots" due to the complexity of trying to do this research while being in touch with the politics of my identity and difference. As I peel the layers one by one, my identity politics presented complications as I engaged in cross-cultural research. The politics of representation is problematic because of how my "body", my ethnicity and race was read; it shifted and had different meaning in various geographical locations. In Canada, I am a racialized being. As a visible minority Canadian, I consider myself part of the Black community, but in Ghana I was considered a foreigner and placed in the "other" category. These identity politics were problematic because my identity is a racialized or visible minority woman in both places, but I was not perceived through this lens in both places. However, this was the space that I began conceptualizing the creation of the *Conscious Career Elevation* model because I began to feel different kinds of embodied tensions that shifted with the varied situations encountered.

In the particular Ghanaian township I was in, at times as a woman I did feel a sense of empowerment from the female respondents because many of them made a point to let me know that the Director of their governing body was a female. Mentioned earlier, the contradiction to that was that other female respondents admitted to having to sacrifice the notion of a family to be in school administration, or had to wait and struggle for many years to have the chance to be promoted. The issue of maternity leave for education professionals in Ghana was important for my journey, I saw women being excluded from promotional opportunities for having children, or not having children due to the strain of finding a replacement during their leave. If they did not produce children in their family, they would feel another kind of situated, gendered ostracization. Some teachers found creative solutions, on the agreement of the principal, a female teacher had her baby tied to her back and taught her lessons. Her students admired her for managing all of her responsibilities. In Ontario, childcare is costly for many; however, due to decades of feminist and labour organizing, we do have policies in place to give new mothers one year maternity leave and even the father could take paternity leave. Despite these supports, I still feel the pressure that women are under to compete for scarce promotional positions. The higher you go in the promotional hierarchy, the more disproportionate the male to female ratio. More women should be able to have access to that escalator of privilege that male elementary school educators have experienced.

The intersections of race and gender to class yielded interesting insights. One of the most challenging activities is engaging in some vast geographical standpoints and entry points around capital. Each country has its own sphere, norms and values around class and capital. It was important for me to hear the voices of individual who were struggling just to eat and sacrificed greatly to attain tertiary education in Ghana, or those in Canada who struggled to gain entry to universities and pay off school loans. These struggles are relative to the country because people have different access and equity viewpoints in each country. It quickly became clear that I had to take each respondent's experience and analyze it in his or her own unique cultural context.

The conversations and the voices were essential for the section on social difference to be analyzed. Highlighted in the sketch of the study, this methodological approach of the narrative or in-depth interviews was necessary because of the personification of the voices in struggle, in triumph, in resiliency, in agency, in subjection, in their power, in their privilege, or in their disappointment and denial of opportunity. The observational dimension of the research was important as well. For all of the interviews, I was able to see and try to understand the respondents in their own frame of reference and in their own professional context only by being in their country and communities. Interviewees shared resources, stories, experiences and professional practices with me. There was a give and take; for both the researcher and the respondents. Many wanted to share their opinions and have a conversation after about the survey to debrief about their experience.

These observational dimensions of the research could not have been reached if there was not the use of narratives or in-depth interviews. However, for the leadership, politics and career mobility portion, the request that the interviewees indicate through a ranking system the relevance of certain attributes was useful for developing a sense of the comparative experiences and perspectives, within the two national groups but primarily between them. I was reluctant to use a ranking system question such as this since such approaches can hide much detail. However, when used in combination with in-depth interviews it proved to be a useful resource in the study. The ranking questions in the survey helped to shape the Conscious Career Elevation (CCE) model, as well as add certainty to the attributes that led to success for the thirty respondents.

Implications of the Study

Generating new directions in career theory, the transdisciplinary approach (Arthur, Hall & Lawrence, 1989) speaks to the cross-rotational job function: gaining experience in multiple positions in different levels of the job. This is a recent development in career theory which will increase an employee's skills and knowledge-base for promotion. I have hoped that this study would contribute to a new research direction for career theory. Rather than career mobility being thought of as a vertical lift or shift in one's career, there are other alternatives, but the value of these alternatives is situational. Horizontal mobility is a progression towards mastery whether it is a shift to mastering a grade or subject, or to another position such as resource teacher position. The functionality of the *Conscious Career Elevation* model is addressing the possibility of both modes of career mobility to be valued.

The trait factor theory created by Nancy Betz (1989) is the closest research related to the types of interests expressed in this study. However, I attempt to go further by identifying specific attributes or characteristics that are needed for success such as political astuteness, higher education, job rotation and others that emerged. This study provides a common set of attributes, qualifications, acumen and experiences that an aspiring educator can refer to in planning career mobility. As we have seen, different forms of capital are implicated, and these concepts draw attention to the accumulation process, and in many cases, suggest barriers to accumulation of these different types of resources based on structural as well as internalized barriers. In other words, from the research, testimonies and lived experiences of education administrators have divulged certain professional navigational actions that one needs to know, in order to avoid the many pitfalls that are built into the system for visible minorities and women.

The Conscious Career Elevation model is an interdisciplinary model. It seeks to contribute to the fields of sociology and equity, education leadership and administration, organizational development, career education, international comparative education and others. The CCE Model is to be used not simply as a mode of analysis, but also as an enabler for change. It has the potential to raise awareness of the complex dynamics of the built-in barriers in the education system, and the roles and choices of action that every educator makes. Choices that people make in terms of where they focus their energies can either empower or disempower, deeply shaping the possibilities of career advancement.

> The possibility for career advancement must be focused on and rooted in personal agency and systemic resiliency for marginalized groups to increase *representation* in school leadership.

In relation to the broader implications for this study to different bodies of literature, I have identified nine key areas worthy of further investigation based on the analysis in this dissertation. I hope these findings will guide further research in social difference, leadership and career mobility. The areas that I feel need further, future attention in the research based on the findings of this study are as follows.

1. Replicate and investigate similar themes of marginalization in career mobility in high school administration across Canada and Ghana. Many more school principals will have to be studied to determine whether the features in elementary schools that emerged will apply. The factors that contribute to marginalized aspiring educators' success identified in this study need to be examined in greater depth so that educators can understand them more fully and apply them in appropriate contexts.

2. Replicate and investigate similar themes of marginalization in career mobility in elementary school administration in other countries such as United States and India that have similar demographics as the countries in this study. Many more school principals will have to be studied to determine whether the features in elementary schools that

emerged will apply. Language difference and contextual modifications may help to assist this process.

3. Investigate further the processes that explain why there are social difference barriers that exist in the education system, and examine why there are limited policies around promotional opportunities within school boards.

4. Analyze the Conscious Career Elevation (CCE) model and explore other models for career advancement and apply it to anti-oppressive pedagogies and frameworks such as anti-racist theory, critical feminist theory, etc. There is a need to develop theory around oppression and career mobility.

5. Given the prominence of staff development and leadership training in school boards, an interesting research focus can be how we integrate in principal, superintendent and director training about how unconscious or conscious oppressive actions may be keeping out many talented marginalized individuals outside of leadership positions. Could an opportunity be created to have a forum to hear the voices of the community that this kind of oppression is happening to?

6. Further lines of inquiry for furthering our understanding of how race, class and gender impede career mobility and how empowerment and resilient tools could assist in the transcendence of this barrier.

7. Due to the changing nature of organizational politics, how can this work inform socio-cultural populations to stay abreast of their social power and limitation; even while in a system that reproduces inequality and helps promote human capital, even if the nature of the entry points of the system and its privilege changes?

8. Because of the randomization of the sample, it would be interesting to see how the results would change and how the voices would change if the sample size consisted of only marginalized individuals. However, it would silence the voice of privilege but, in turn, it would personify the voice of the struggle and perhaps, in effect, have more depth in terms of narrative.

9. Investigate further isolating one variable of social difference such as race. How would that change the outcome? Can it be representative of a person with multi-oppressions in their identity? For example, how would the study change if it reflected varied ability and sexuality too? Particularly, if intersectionality has "blind spots" then, how can one

isolate an oppressive part of one's own identity, and still have his or her full identity represented? This is a notion to explore.

Flowing With the Stream

Having now reached the end of my study, what does this study mean to me? As a visible minority female elementary educator who is interested in school leadership promotion and who is committed to the profession of education, this research experience has enriched my understanding of others who have the same aspirations and have made it.

> It was important to hear their struggles, as well as understanding the voices of privilege and learning from them the structures and social nuances that define career success.

This research responds to some of my deepest passions, the barriers in one's professional life and knowing how to overcome them. These barriers are embedded within institutions that mutually inform one another through situational mirrors such as race, gender and socio-economic status.

For most of my life, I have been involved within the educational context, teaching at various levels and within several different countries. Throughout my experience, I had to navigate systems to "climb the education ladder." In my climbing, it became apparent to me that race, gender and other social differences interrupted processes of mobility. I often wondered how it could be easier for marginalized groups including visible minority women to gain career mobility, since it was expressed as difficult, and at times impossible. I wondered what they would need to know in order to navigate the global education system. With this in mind, the results and use of the ten agency attributes empower an educator's career.

It was my hope that anecdotal and narrative interviews, survey-styled questions and observation, and attempts at triangulation would support marginalized individuals and communities as they begin their educational careers. What I did not expect as I embarked on this journey was that mobility would be complicated to the degree that it is by the political ramifications of the initial barriers that marginalized groups including visible minority women face when initiating their career. I began to realize that the possible impact of these initial barriers can be de-energizing for marginalized groups, resulting in a loss of motivation to advance within the education system. At this point, I began to wonder if marginalized groups dropped out or were pushed out from decision-making power, and how these processes are instrumental in exclusionary systemic silencing.

By starting with myself as text, I explored from my own experience of race, gender, age, class and human, social and cultural capital processes, and how career mobility could be limiting for marginalized groups. It was important to understand what can be done to counter the barriers, and howBy starting with myself as text, I explored from my own experience of race, gender, age, class and human, social and cultural capital processes, and how career mobility could be limiting for marginalized groups. It was important to understand what can be done to counter the barriers, and how strategy can allow for marginalized groups including visible minority women to have a voice in international education.

The other layer to this study was that it was a cross-cultural study. It gave me contradicting and connecting experience to my personal history. Ghana is where my parent's island of Trinidad and Tobago's ancestry is from (the Middle Passage). Through this study, I can shed some light and perspective on occupational injustices and inequities surrounding marginalized professionals and promotion. This new knowledge of the Conscious Career Elevation model, the findings and navigational tools are all for internalized empowerment and systemic resiliency. I think it is uplifting to see the creativity and determination that marginalized individuals and women specifically have generated to endure and to attain higher levels in their careers across both countries.

There are many empowering tools that were elicited from the principals I interviewed in both Ghana and Ontario. Through the sharing of ideas and experiences, dialogues and conversations, research and readings, I discovered there are ten common identifiable characteristics involved in career mobility in education. The academic, social, political and emotional development of an individual are addressed. Professional development has a symbiotic relationship with leadership, they go hand in hand. Leadership and personality are intertwined.

The Conscious Career Elevation (CCE) model recognizes the intersectionalities of the politics of identity in complex yet small steps towards greater, strategic consciousness. The elementary school system is quite unique in that the demographics of the teacher population in both countries that I looked at, but diversity are not fully represented at the levels of school administrators or superintendents. The number of female educators is significantly higher than males, yet the males dominate the administration ranks by virtue of informal networks otherwise known as the old boys' network and nepotism and other forms of inequitable access to opportunity and resources. This leaves progressive women teaching professionals to compete against each other.

This competitive versus cooperative professional environment can foster the image and mentality of not simply doggedness but the idea of an individualistic "survival of the fittest" attitude. Women are not seen as helping each other along as much as perhaps they could.

As a result, most Canadian respondents felt like we can or must climb on our own, but as the Ghanaian community's example taught us, collective advancement and giving a professional a boost up the ladder through sharing information, mentorship, advice, knowledge, politics and power dynamics within an organization, is vital to the collective representation of any group.

Career mobility is often conceptualized as a vertical progression within one's career development. We are constantly reminded of where we have been, and the barriers that still must be overcome. But we must also be aware of the continual barriers the journey will incur, and the characteristics we needs to develop to help climb to that next step; because the historical barriers of the education system are fighting minoritized individuals every step of the way.

When one does reach another career destination, to sustain that achievement is imperative. To be consistent and capable in the new responsibilities and managing change is important for the next progression and for assisting others in rising through the ranks as well. When moving upward, we must constantly hone our skills and improve personal competence. This is central to our own realization process and career advancement. In both Ghana and Ontario, the education system rapidly changes daily and it is crucial to stay informed and to be adept when attempting to make some career moves. In contrast, some view the transition from teacher to principal to be another job entirely, that the position of principal does not have many of the same characteristics as the position of teacher. Thus, it is more of a career change than a progression. Seeing that most administrators are required to attain five or more years of experience to facilitate, advise and govern a school and staff, the role and responsibilities of teachers are interwoven in the delivery of administrative duties.

This study gives a situational context to how we can use these ten identifiable characteristics to create upward mobility opportunities for ourselves.

> This study's purpose was to empower an individual who experiences social difference inequalities including race and gender with a new lens of viewing the system; and to point out that it is possible to stay within the system and navigate your career to shift barriers using personal agency, systemic resiliency and *finding allies in the system.*

People skills, good relationship with management, gaining high visibility assignments, having influential mentors and creating personal style, are all important in one's understanding of emotional intelligence and its role in the use-value of social capital in one's career mobility within their organization. Daniel Goleman explains that self-awareness, managing emotions and motivating oneself marshal "emotions in the service of a goal, is essential for paying attention, for self-motivation and mastery, and for creativity". He states the art of relationships is, in a large part, skill in managing emotions in others. When we look at social competence, these abilities reveal themselves as the abilities that under-gird popularity, leadership, and interpersonal effectiveness. People who excel in these skills do well at anything that relies on interacting smoothly with others, they are social stars. (Goleman, 1995) This broadens the scope of the interactions at play within a school board and a school. A school is a microcosm of the education system at large, seeing the network, being included or excluded, having information or not being privy to it are all areas that need improvement for all to advance in the education system. To extend this idea further is to understand that global education systems have similar barriers and problems embedded in them, and that some of these problems are not yet brought to light. An educator can benefit both politically and personally by seeing this problem as unifying, and that this universal problem is now being recognized by progressive educators around the globe to combat its oppressive nature.

> After this analysis of career mobility, how are marginalized groups including women and visible minorities identity supposed to *"make it"* in this context? The tangible answer that arose for this journey is finding allies, personal resilience and agency, and structural transformation.

In white water rafting, it is important that you do not use a canoe. Instead you want to be in connection with others on the proper boat, with the proper gear, ready to enjoy the calm and the rough waters, which can also be exciting when skillfully handled. Navigating choppy waters is always best when we remember our purpose, and why we chose to go on this journey. The journey can be stressful but if all of us can hold on to the bigger reason for embarking on this journey, that reason can hold us together when waters are rough. When in touch with purpose and connection, the navigation is possible. It is also good to remember that we will have differences, not only in our backgrounds, but personally and in terms of our views on how we should move for change, how we should move through the waters. It is important to ask what might be influencing ours or a person's way of being; sometimes it is our particular life experience. The other notion is to not assume disconnection with others who we think are not aligned with us. What I mean by this is that I have been surprised at where I have found my allies and where I have not. Sometimes our allies are not who we expect.

> It's good to think of this when sitting at a table with so called 'people in suits'. Some of them may be your allies more than you know. You do not know what they are doing behind the scenes. They may be being strategic and not saying much at the meetings. Don't assume you know the player's hand, similar to poker; there are activists in all settings, moving carefully. Also, treat everyone as a potential ally, and see what happens. When invited into a dance of support, rather than fear, miracles can happen. (Vinsky, 2010)

Structural transformation or role transcendence needs to be addressed because the system is built with pitfalls and barriers such as race, gender and other social differences. An example of transcending racism would be the establishment of a committee backed by the school board, which executes policies to combat racial incidents and situations.

Being prepared for the endurance, resilience and agency needed to transcend systemic barriers is imperative to rising in your career. We must be critical of the system to triumph over these barriers, and shift our perspectives about career mobility. When I was reading some of the literature on career, the question came up, "does this literature understand the complexity of marginality?" and "who does this career theory cater to?" "Is there truly access and equity to the higher level positions?" I am writing this for all the levels of marginalization including those that my identity represents: minority cultures, young women, class status and other social difference. It is important to shift the barriers in the education system, in order for all marginalized groups to have a say.

Comparing marginalized identities against the rating of the ten attributes of career mobility as they were chosen in order of importance in both Ghana and Canada can help us to realize the specific barriers faced. Gender becomes quite salient in a particular country or cultural capital in another. There are unique yet overlapping similarities within the two countries that international educators can capitalize on.

> The expectation was not to create a formula for "how to make it" in the education system, rather it was to unite global educators with the attributes that left an imprint on how to be successful in education preparation and promotion.

The preparation is to understand one's specific identity as well as the education system and its recognized personal pattern of individual progression. Moreover, to learn, choose and utilize the identifiable characteristics in the Conscious Career Elevation Model that works for your own particular circumstance and put them into practice.

Additionally, look at what particular barrier you, the aspiring educator is currently facing and understand how it is being interrupted in the education system. How is the cycle of marginality interrupting one's path or plan for upward mobility? It is a point of reckoning when we analyze our own authentic experience and realize, for example, "I have been pushed out not dropped out." (Dei, 2006) This conclusion is similar to how some of the visible minority youth experience many of the same barriers in the education system when trying to attain their academic goals. Can we navigate our career to gain decision-making power to interrupt the same cycle that has been keeping one back?

Is the initial process of entering the system compounded with barriers that are actually designed to shut out certain people? Moreover, how is the system blocking the voice of marginalized peoples? Thus, if the initial process of trying to establish leadership is exclusionary, and is designed to drown out the voice of marginalized groups including visible minorities and women, then what are the long-term implications for our current visible minority students and girls who aspire to be educators, principals and beyond? The implications are professional abandonment, being shut out or developing health concerns. Professional abandonment is the abandonment or lack of support of the individual educator in the system, causing the educator to feel forced to leave the education system and venture into another profession. Shutting an educator out means pushing her out of powerful positions and influence, therefore, the alternative voices are silenced in decision-making power. Health concerns of the body, mind and soul are other implications. If we do not recognize how the system interrupts educators for their race, gender or other social differences, then the long-term effects implicate a standstill in the progressive movement we need to make in our education system; we need diverse decision-making power.

This is a critical time for Canada, Ghana and the world to look at systemic barriers and look at the impact it has on marginalized voices in any specific community. This kind of formalized research aims to identify the factors of the interruption process in career mobility, in order to begin to deconstruct this exclusionary process. By using oneself as text as an aspiring leader and developing possible criteria for mobility in the education system, administrators, school board personnel and teachers can use this information to interrupt the systemic process that can shut people out and can sustain a system of dominance. The natural process of motivation and determination needed for promotion becomes interrupted time and time again. This research gives us some direction to help the individual understand the systemic aspect of the barriers she may personally face. It also highlights systemic processes that can obstruct mobility for marginalized groups to gain decision-making power such as exclusion, sabotage, asynchronic power relations, and the lack of access to information and informal networks, etc. Further formal exploration can solidify the characteristics or traits that assist in the career mobility process.

This research study is for all marginalized groups including visible minorities, women, and other social differences in the system who aspire to go into the field of school leadership and beyond. However, it is not limited to the context of educational work alone. It is transferable to many fields and disciplines. My personal goal in this study was to give voice to those powerful educators and aspiring leaders that are currently being marginalized. The abyss of self-closure is a re-birth of empowerment.

Speaking truth to power has never been an easy task; however, I believe the Conscious Career Elevation model will serve as an empowerment tool for many silenced voices.

Be heard!
Have resiliency!
Maintain leadership!
Create tension!
Find allies!
Transcend barriers!
Gain self-empowerment!

AFTERWORD

Throughout the history of Canada and in many Africa nations including Ghana and Kenya, many minoritized groups and in particular, women have not benefited fully from the education system. There is, therefore, a need to create spaces for marginalized groups both in Canada and elsewhere. It is important to reclaim spaces that acknowledge and speak to the contributions of African-Canadians to the education systems. The author of *Bridging the Opportunity Gap* must be applauded for taking bold initiative to outline and speak to the contributions of people of African descents to the education system in Canada. Sadly, in spite of these contributions, there are fewer opportunities given to people of African descents to give more to the education system. The book, while outlining the contributions of people of African descents to the Canadian school system, is also reminding us that more opportunities need to be provided to marginalized groups to contribute more to the education system.

The book also reminds us there are material investments in the oppression of others and these investments allow people who are gaining from structures of oppression to serve as gate-keepers and gate-crashers to any effort to have structural changes. For the author, the real victims of these gate-keepings and gate-crashings are our children and future generation who see the promise of education slipping away every day. Today, there are Occupy movements speaking about the increasing gaps between the one percent and the ninety-nine percents. Yet, the discussion about the one percent cannot be completed if educators are not willing to talk about the ninety-nine percent; especially, the seemingly increasing gaps even among the nine-nine percent. The book is a reminder that there must be a place in education where self-reflexivity and self-engagement is encouraged. Frantz Fanon asks: Have I not because of what I have done or failed to do contribute to the oppression of others and my oppression?

Bridging the Opportunity Gap is invariably asking similar question but this time, it is a question that demands answers. Answers that will renew hope of education. They are answers that will not trivialize the questions of quantitative and qualitative representation of minoritized groups in the education system.

I believe all marginalized groups including African-Canadian women need to carve out a critical space to talk about their work and their realities, to mobilize in order to increase and to make visible change in the demographics of school leadership. In other words, how do we deconstruct a self-perpetuating pattern based on the values, interests and views of the dominant forces in the education system? I think that as a starting point, whether coming from another country, or this very familiar location, colonial and neo-colonial practices disturb and disorient our sense of race, class, gender, sexual orientation and ability that can open up discussion on colonial thought using our identity as a reference point. What emerges are voices, desires and bodies of knowledge that reveal a sense of culture, of politics, history and identity that can no longer be denied when promotion is being determined whether through our own self-referential analysis as an educator or through the powers that be. The author of this book has shown the way; let the rest of us follow.

Bridging the Opportunity Gap encourages dialogue that is two-prong. The first, for the marginalized educator, who through the deconstruction of colonial thought in self-referential analysis, opens up the thought of the aspiration for education leadership promotion. This book outlines ten agency attributes to give resiliency and empowerment to those who experience or perceive "impenetrable" barriers in the education systems where they reside and form their lived social reality. The second, for the individuals on education leadership hiring committees, a revelation based on new cultural, political, historical and personal identity can cause a shift in employment hiring practices that promotes the real possibility of having proportionate demographic representation of student to school leadership. This book is a must for all educators who advocate for equity and social justice.

Njoki Nathani Wane, Ph.D.
Professor,
Ontario Institute for Studies in Education,
University of Toronto

REFERENCES

Acker, J. (1990). Hierarchies, Jobs, Bodies: A Theory of Gendered Organizations. *Gender and Society, 4, 2*,p. 147.

Acker, S., Dillabough, J. (2007). Women "Learning to Labour" in the "Male Emporium": Exploring Gendered Work in Teacher Education. *Gender and Education, 19, 3*, 297-316.

Adams, Maurianne, Lee Anne Bell and Pat Griffen. (1997). *Teaching For Diversity and Social Justice.* New York, NY: Routledge.

Akyeampong, K. (2003). *Teacher Training in Ghana-Does It Count?* Multi-Site teacher Education Research Project (MUSTER), London: DFID.p. ix.

Alderfer C.P. (1989). *Learning from Changing: Organizational Diagnosis and Development.* London: SAGE Publications.

Anderson, S.E. & Sonia Ben Jaafar., (2003). *Policy Trends in Ontario Education (1990-2003)*, March, 2006, from http://fcis.oise.utoronto.ca/~icec/policytrends.pdf (2006) http://www.tcdsb.org/history.html

Anyon, J. (1985). Social Class and School Knowledge Revisited: A Reply to Ramsay. And P.D.K. Ramsay, Social Class and School Knowledge: A Rejoinder to Jean

Anyon. *Curriculum Inquiry 15, 1*, 209-222.

Apple, M. (1971). The hidden curriculum and the nature of conflict. *Interchange, 11, 4*, 27-40.

Apple, M. (1979). *Ideology and the curriculum.* London: Routledge & Kegan Paul.

Arber, R. (2000). "Defining Positioning within Politics of Difference: Negotiating Spaces 'in between.' *Race, Ethnicity and Education 3, 1*, 46.

Arendt, H. (1970). *Communicative Power.* In S.Lukes (Ed.). London: Basil Blackwell.

Arnove, R.F. and C.A. Torres (Eds.). (2003). Comparative Education: The Dialectic of the Global and the Local. Cambridge, Oxford: Rowman and Littlefield Publishers.

Arthur, M., D. Hall & B. Lawrence. (1989). *Handbook of Career Theory*. Oxford, Cambridge: Cambridge University Press. p. 7

Bailey, G. & N. Gayle. (2003). *Ideology: Structuring Identities in Contemporary Life*. Peterborough: Broadview Press.

Ball, S. J. (2003). *Class strategies and the education market: The middle class and social advantage*. New York, NY: Routledge. p. 3

Barbara Herring & Associates. (2007). Demographic Composition of Toronto District School Board Employees. TDSB Workforce Census. P. 17-18

Beck, U. (1992). *Risk Society: Towards a new modernity*. London: Sage.

Beck, U. (1999). *World Risk Society*. Cambridge: Polity.

Becker, G. (1964). *Human Capital: A Theoretical and Empirical Analysis, with Special Reference to Education*. Chicago: University of Chicago Press.

Becker, G. (1993). *Human Capital*. (3rd Ed.). Chicago: University of Chicago Press.

Becker, G. (1994). *Human Capital: A Theoretical and Empirical Analysis With Special Reference to Education*. Chicago: The University of Chicago Press.

Beem, C. (1999). The Necessity of Politics, Reclaiming American public life. Chicago: University of Chicago Press.

Bell, D and Treiman. (1973). *The Coming of Post-Industrial Society: A Venture in Social*

Bernstein, B. (1971). *Class, Codes and Control, Vol. I*. London: Routledge and Kegan

Bernstein, B. (1990). *The Structuring of Pedagogic Discourse*. London: Routledge.

Beyer, L. E. & d. D. P. Liston, (1992). Discourse or moral action? A critique of postmodernism. *Educational Theory, 42*, 371-393.

Bhavnani, Kum-Kum and Ann Phoenix. (1994). *Shifting Identities Shifting Racisms: A Feminism and Psychology Reader*. London: SAGE Publications.

Billett, S. (2001). Learning through working life: interdependencies at work. *Studies in Continuing Education, 23, 1*, 19–35.

Biology Online., (2006). *Career*. April, 2006, from www.biology-online. org/dictionary/career

Bivens, D., (1995). *Women's Theological Center – Evaluation Tools for Racial Equity-Internalized Racism: A Definition*. October, 2005, from http://www.evaluation toolsforracialequity.org/termRacial.htm and http://www.thewtc.org /Internalized_Racism.pdf p.1

Blakely, E. J. and Synder, M. G. (1997). *Fortress America: Gated communities in the United States*. Washington DC: Brookings Institute.

Blasé & Blasé, J.. (1989). The micropolitics of the school. The everyday political orientation of teachers toward open school principals. *Educational Administration Quarterly, 25, 5*, p. 391.

Blase, J. (1991). The micropolitical orientation of teachers toward closed school principals. *Education and Urban Society, 23, 4*, 356-378.

Blaug, M. (1987). Declining subsidies in tertiary education: An economic analysis. In M. Blaug, (Ed.) *The Economics of Education and the Education of an Economist*. New York: New York University Press.

Blaug, M. (1987). Rate of return on investment in Great Britain. In M. Blaug (Ed.) *The Economics of Education and the Education of an Economist*. New York: New York University Press.

Block, F. (1990). *Post Industrial Possibilities: A Critique of Economic Discourse*. Los Angeles: University of California Press.

Bloomer, M. & Hodkinson, P. (2000). "Learning careers: continuity and change in young people's dispositions to learning" *British Journal of Educational Studies, 26* (5): 583–598.

Boeckmann, R.J. Feather, N.T, (2007). Gender, Discrimination Beliefs, Group-Based Guilt, and Responses to Affirmative Action for Australian Women. *Psychology of Women Quarterly, 31, 3*, 290-304.

Bookman, A. (2004). Starting in our own backyards. How working families can build community and survive the new economy. New York: Routledge.

Bolman, L.G.& Deal, T.E. (1991). *Reframing Organizations: Artistry, Choice and Leadership*. San Francisco: Jossey-Bass. p.449

Bourdieu, P. (1973) "Cultural reproduction and social reproduction" in R. Brown (Ed.) *Knowledge, Education and Cultural Change*. London: Tavistock.

Bourdieu, P. and J-C. Passeron. (1977*). Reproduction in Education, Society and Culture*. London: SAGE Publications.

Bourdieu, P. and J. Passeron. (1979). *The Inheritors*. Chicago: University of Chicago Press.

Bourdieu, P. (1983). Forms of capital. In J. C. Richards (Ed.). *Handbook of Theory and Research for the Sociology of Education*. New York: Greenwood Press.

Bourdieu, P. (1984). *Distinction: A Social Critique of the Judgement of Taste*. London: Routledge & Keegan Paul.

Bourdieu, P. (1986). The forms of capital (Trans. R.Nice). In J. Richardson (Ed.), *Handbook and research for the sociology of education*. New York, NY: Greenwood Press.

Bourdieu, P. & Wacquant, L. (1992). *An Invitation to Reflexive Sociology*. Cambridge: Polity Press.

Bourdieu, P. (1998) *Practical Reason*. Cambridge, Oxford: Polity Press.

Bowles, S. & H. Gintas. (1976). *Schooling in Capitalist America*. London: Routledge and Kegan Paul.

Brand, D. (1999). Black Women and Work: The Impact of Racially Constructed Gender Roles on the Sexual Division of Labour in E. Dua and A. Robertson (Eds.), *Scratching the Surface: Canadian Anti-Racist, Feminist Thought*. Toronto: Women's Press.

Braverman, H. (2001). *Labor and Monopoly Capitalism*.

Brewer, R. (1994). *Theorizing Race, Class and Gender: The New Scholarship of Black Feminist Intellectuals and Black Feminisms: The Visionary Pragmatism of Black Women*. New York, NY: Routledge.

Brine, J. (1999). Undereducating Women: globalizing inequality. Buckingham: Open University Press.

Buah, F.K. (1998). *The History of Ghana*. Oxford: MacMillan Education. p. 20

Bulmer, Martin and John Solomos (Eds.). (2004). *Researching Race and Racism*. London: Routledge.

Burack, C. (2004). *Healing Identities: Black Feminist Thought and The Politics of Groups*. Ithaca, NY: Cornell University Press.

Burris, B. (1983). *No Room at the Top: Underemployment and Alienation in the Corporation*. New York, NY: Praeger Publishers.

Business Balls., (2006). *Leadership Developmental Tips*. November, 2006, from http://www.businessballs.com/

Callahan, J. Tomaszewski, L. (2007). Navigating the Good Ol' Boys Club: Women, Marginality, and Communities of Practice in a Military Non-Profit Organization. *Studies in Continuing Education, 29, 3, 59-276.*

Carnoy & Levin, (1985), *Schooling and work in the democratic state*. Stanford University Press. p. 993.

Carr, P. R. and Thomas Klassen. (1995) *The Role of Racial Minority Teachers in Anti-racist Education.* Toronto. pp. 126-138.

Carr, Paul. (1995) "Employment Equity for Racial Minorities in the Teaching Profession." *Multicultural Education Journal,* Volume 13, Number 1:28-42.

Carter, B. (1997). The Restructuring of Teaching and the Restructuring of Class. *British Journal of Sociology of Education 18, 1,* 201-215.

Castanga, M. and G. J. S., Dei (2000). "An historical overview of the application of the race concept in social practice." In A. Calliste & G. S. Dei, (Eds.). *Anti-racist feminism: Critical race and gender studies.* Halifax, NS: Fernwood.

Central Intelligence Agency., (2006). *The World Factbook Ghana.* January, 2006, from http://www.cia.gov./cia/publications/factbook/.

Cheng, Maisy L. (1987a) *Visible Minority Representation in the Toronto Board of Education: Staff Changes, 1986.* (Research Report #183). Toronto: Toronto Board of Education.
(1987b)*Who Seeks the Work? A Pre-Employment Pilot Survey.* (Research Report #184). Toronto: Toronto Board of Education. p.21, 27
(1987c)*Representation of Visible/Racial Minorities in the Toronto Board of Education Work Force, 1987.* (Research Report #186). Toronto: Toronto Board of Education.

Christiansen, C. H. and Townsend, E. A. (2004). *Introduction to Occupation-The Art and Science of Living.* Upper Sadler River, NY: Prentice Hall.

Cohen, D. and Prusak, L. (2001). *In Good Company: How social capital makes organizations work.* Boston, Ma.: Harvard Business School Press. p. 10

Coleman, J. C. (1988). Social capital in the creation of human capital. *American Journal of Sociology, 94,* S95-S120.

Coleman, J. C. (1994). *Foundations of Social Theory.* Cambridge, Mass.: Harvard University Press. p. 302

Collins, R. (1979). *The Credentialing Society: An Historical Sociology of Education and Stratification.* New York: Academic Press.

Connolly, P. (1992). Playing it by the Rules: The Politics of Research in 'Race' and Education. *British Educational Research* Journal 18, 2, 133-148.

Coolahan, J. (2004). The Development of Educational Studies and Teacher Education. University of Western Australia. *Education Research & Perspectives Journal 31, 2, 32.*

Cormier, J. (2004). The impact of Movements: Bureaucratic Insurgency, Canadianization and the CSAA. *The Canadian Review of Sociology and Anthropology 41, 2.*

Cornish, K. (1977). *The Jew of Linz: Wittgenstein, Hitler and their secret battle for the mind.* Century Books.

Crawford, C. (2004). African Caribbean Women, Diaspora and Transnationality. *Canadian Woman's Studies: Women and the Black Diaspora 23, 2,* 97-103.

Crwys-Williams, J. (1997) In the words of nelson Mandela: A Little Pocketbook. South Africa: Penguin Books. p.35

Currie, Janice. (2006). Response. *Canada: Educational Administration I:* Web Knowledge Forum.

Daniel, B-J. (2005). Researching African Canadian Women: Indigenous Knowledges and the Politics of Representation. In Dei, G. J. S. and G. Johal (Eds.). *Critical Issues in Anti-Racist Research Methodology.* New York, NY: Peter Lang Publishing.

Das Gupta, T. (1996). *Racism & Paid Work.* Aurora ON: Garamond Press.

Davies, S. and N. Guppy. (1998).Race and Canadian Education. In V. Satzewich. *Racism and Social Inequality in Canada.* Toronto: Thompson Educational Publishing Inc. *Statistics cited Unpublished data from Census Analysis Division, 1991 Census, Statistics Canada.*

Day, C. (1998). Working with the Different Selves of Teachers: Beyond Comfortable Collaboration. *Educational Action Research 6, 2,* 255–273.

De Tocqueville, A. (1994). *Democracy in America.* London: Fontana Press.

Deci, E.L. (1996). *Why we do what we do :Understanding self motivation.* London: Penguin.

Dei, G. J. S. (1996). *Anti Racism Education.* Halifax, NS: Fernwood.

Dei, G. J. S. and A. Ashgharzadeh. (2001). The Power of Social Theory: Towards an Anti-Colonial Discursive Framework. *Journal of Education Thought 35, 3,* p. 305.

Dei, G. and Johal, G. (2005). *Critical Issues in Anti-Racist Research Methodologies.* New York, NY: Peter Lang Publishing. p.53.

Dei, G. J. S. (2006). Interview with George Dei –Primary, Secondary and Tertiary Education Systems in Ghana. March 20. University of Toronto/ OISE: Toronto.

Delgado, R. & A. K. Wing. (2003). *Critical Race Feminism.* (2nd Ed.) New York, NY: New York University Press.

Deng, F.M. (1985). Learning in Context: An African Perspective, in A. Thomas and E.T. Ploman (Eds.), *Learning and Development in a Global Perspective.* (pp. 90-107) Toronto: OISE Press.

Dictionary by Labor Law Talk., (2006). *Human Capital.* October, 2006, from http://dictionary.laborlawtalk.com/Human_capital.

Diop, C.A. (1997). *The African Origin of Civilization.* Westport, CT: Lawrence Hill.

DiPrete. T. (1990). Adding Covariates to Loglinear Models for the Study of Social Mobility." *American Sociological Review, 55,* 757-773.

Dolphyne, F.A. (1991). *The Emancipation of Women: An African Persepctive.* Accra: Ghana University Press. p. x, xi, 49

Downey, C. J. (1998). Is it time for us to be accountable too *The AASA Professor 22, 1,* 12-16.

Dubois, W.E.B. (1903). *The Souls of Black Folks.* New York, NY: Fine Media and Creative Media Inc.

Duany, A., Plater-Zyberk, E. and Speck, J. (2000). *Suburban Nation: The Rise of Sprawl and the Decline of the American Dream.* New York: North Point Press.

Eagly, A.H. (2007). Female Leadership Advantage and Disadvantage: Resolving the Contradictions. *Psychology of Women Quarterly, 31, 1,* 1-12.

Edwards, Michael. (2004). *Civil Society.* Cambridge: Polity.

Elster, J. (1983). *Sour Grapes. Studies in the Subversion of Rationality.* Cambridge: Cambridge University Press.

Engelstrom, Y. (1999) Activity theory and individual and social transformation in Y. Engelstrom, R. Miettinen & R. Punamaki (Eds.) *Perspectives on Activity Theory* Cambridge, Oxford: Cambridge University Press.

Engelstrom, Y. (2001). Expansive Learning at Work: Towards an Activity-Theoretical Reconceptualisation. *Journal of Education and Work, 14, 1,* 133–156.

En La Lucha, H. and Sampaio, A. (2004). Transnational Feminisms in a New Global Matrix. *International Feminist Journal of Politics, 6, 2,* 181-206.

Erikson, R. & J. Goldthrope. (1992). *The Constant Flux: A Study of Class Mobility in Industrial Societies.* Cambridge, Oxford: Clarendon Press.

Essed, P. (1991). *Understanding Everyday Racism: An Interdisciplinary Theory.* Newbury Park: SAGE Publications..p. 14, 39, 40, 136

European Union Ministry of Education. (2006). *Human Capital.* January, 2006, from *http://ec.europa.eu/employment social/knowledge society/ conf en.htm*

Eyerman, R. (2001). *Cultural Trauma-Slavery and the Formation of African American Identity.* Cambridge, Oxford: Cambridge University Press.

Fagerlind, I. & L. J. Saha (1989). *Education and National Development: A Comparative Perspective (2nd Ed.).* Toronto: Pergamon.

Fanon, F. (1963). *The Wretched of the Earth.* New York, NY: Grove Weidenfeld.

Field, J. (2003). *Social Capital.* London: Routledge, p. 42

Fenwick, T. (2001). Tides of Change: New Themes and Questions in Workplace Learning. New Directions for Adult and Continuing Education.

Fine, M. and Virginia Vanderslice. (1991). Qualitative Activist Research: Reflections on Politics and Methods in Bryant, F. B. et. Al. (Eds.). *Methodological Issues in Applied Social Psycholgy.* New York, NY: Plenum. p. 206

Fine, B. (2000). Social Capital Versus Social Theory: Political Economy and Social Science at the Turn of the Millennium. London: Routledge.

Fisher, R. and W. Ury. (1991). *Getting To Yes: Negotiating Agreement Without Giving In.* New York, NY: Penguin Books.

Fitzsimons, P. & M. Peters. (1994). Human capital theory and the Government's Industry Training Strategy. *Journal of Education Policy, 9, 3,* 245-266.

Fitzsimons, P. (1997). Human capital theory and participation in tertiary education. In K-M. Mathews & M. Olssen (Eds.). *Critical Perspectives on Education Policy For the 1990s and Beyond .* Palmerston North: The Dunmore Press.

Fleras, Augie and Jean Leonard Elliott. (1999). *Unequal Relations: An Introduction to Race, Ethnic, and Aboriginal Dynamics in Canada, Third Ed.* Scarborough, ON: Prentice Hall Allyn and Bacon Canada.

Fletcher, J. (1997). Relational Practice: A Feminist Re-construction of Work. *Journal of Management Inquiry, 7.*

Foley, M. W. and Edwards, B. (1999). Is It Time to Disinvest in Social Capital? *Journal of Public Policy 19:2,* 141–73.

Foray, D. & B. Lundvall (1996). The knowledge-based economy: From the economics of knowledge to the learning economy. In *Employment and Growth in the Knowledge-based Economy OECD Documents.* Paris: OECD. p.21

Forrester, K., Payne, J. & Ward, K. (1995) "Lifelong education and the workplace: a critical analysis" *International Journal of Lifelong Education,* 14, 4, 292–305

Foster, W. (1986). *Paradigms and Promises: New Approaches to Educational Administration.* Amherst: Prometheus Books. p. 7

Foster, P. (1990). *Policy and Practice in Multicultural and Anti-Racist Education.* London: Routledge. p. 4

Frankenberg, R. (2004). On Unsteady Ground: Crafting and Engaging in the Critical Study of Whiteness." In Bulmer, Martin and John Solomos (Eds.). *Researching Race and Racism.* London: Routledge.

Frankenberg, R. (1993). *The Social Construction of Whiteness: white women-race matters.* London: Routledge.

Freire, P. (1971). *Pedagogy of the Oppressed.* New York, NY: Herder and Herder.

Freire, P. (1985). *The Politics of Education: Culture, Power and Liberation.* (Trans. D. Macedo). South Hadley, MA: Bergin & Garvey Publishers.

Freire, P. (1998*). Pedagogy of Freedom: Ethics, Democracy and Civic Courage.* Lanham: Rowman & Littlefield.

Freud, Sigmund. (1924). *Collected Papers.* International Psychoanalytic Press.

Friedman, M. (1962). *Capitalism and Freedom.* Chicago: University of Chicago Press.

Fukuyama, F. (1999). The Great Disruption. Human nature and the reconstitution of social order. London: Profile Books.

Fullan, M., Bertani, A., & Quinn, J. (2004). New lessons for district wide reform. *Educational Leadership 61,* 7, 42-46.

Garavan, T.N., and M. Coolahan. (1996). Career Mobility within Organizations: Implications for Career Development. *Journal of European Industrial Training 20, 5,* 31-39.

Ghana Education Service/Ministry of Education. (2006). *Primary Education, Teacher In-Service, Education Policy Planners-Hiring Practice.* January, 2006, from http://www.unesco.org/education /educprog/ste/ network/country/ghana.html, p. 1

Giroux, H.A. (1983). Theories of Reproduction and Resistance in New Sociology of Education. *Harvard Educational Review 53,* 257-293.

Godard, John. (2000). *Industrial Relations, the Economy and Society.* Captus Press.

Goleman, Daniel. (1995). *Emotional Intelligence.* New York, NY: Bantam Books.

Gooch, Peter (2006*). Why are educational institutions prey to administrative fashions? Educational Administration I* Spring 06, Web Knowledge Forum. p. 1

Goodson, I. & Hargreaves, A. (Eds.). (1996). *Teachers' Professional Lives.* London: Falmer Press.

Goyder, J. (2005). The Dynamics of Occupational Prestige: 1975-2005. *The Canadian Review of Sociology and Anthropology 42, 1.*

Grogan, M. & Andrews, R. (2004). Defining preparation and professional development for the future. *Educational Administration Quarterly 38, 2,* p. 235.

Government of Ontario., (2008). *Ontario Budget.,* September 2006, from http://www.ontariobudget.ca /english/index.html

Haidt, J. (2006). The Happiness Hypothesis. Putting ancient wisdom and philosophy to the test of modern science. London: Heinemann.

Hall, R. & B. Sandler, (1982). *The Classroom Climate: a chilly one for women.* Project on the Status and Education of Women, Washington, DC: Association of American Colleges.

Hall, S. (1986). Variants of Liberalism. In J. Donald & S. Hall (Eds.). *Politics and Ideology.* Milton Keyes: Open University Press.

Hall, S. (1996). "Race; the Floating Signifier, Introduction Discussion", Lecture and Criticisms on the Lecture. North Hampton, MA: Media Addition Foundation; introduced by Sutjhally; produced, directed and edited by Sutjhally, Classroom ed. (Video)

Hall, P. (1999). Social capital in Britain. *British Journal of Political Science, 29:3,* 417-61.

Haller, A. & Millers, Irwin. (1972). *The Occupational Aspirations Scale.* Cambridge, MA: Schenkman.

Hanifan, L. J. (1916). The rural school community center. *Annals of the American Academy of Political and Social Science, 67,* 130-138.

Hanifan, L. J. (1920). *The Community Center.* Boston: Silver Burdett.

Hare, W., Portelli, J.P., (2003). *What to Do? Case Studies for Educators.* (3rd Ed.)

Halifax, NS: Edphil Books.p. 25, 43.

Hartung, P. J. (2004) "Cultural context in career theory and practice: role salient and values". *Career Development Quarterly.*

Hatcher, R. (1994). Market relationships and the management of teachers. *British Journal of Sociology of Education 15, 1,* 41-61.

Heifeitz, R. (1994). Leadership Without Easy Answers. Cambridge, MA: The Belknap Press of Harvard University Press. p. 18

Heifeitz, H. & Linsky, Marty. (2002). *Leadership on the Line.* Boston, MA: Harvard Business School Press. p. 160, 204

Heifeitz, H. & Linsky, Marty. (2006). When *Leadership Spells D A N G E R.* Boston, MA: Harvard Business School Press. p. 35

Henderson, R.E. (1992). *The Last White Rose: the white race, survival of oblivion.* Nowra Instant Printing: Australia.

Henry, A. (1998). Possibilities and Limitations of Oppositional Standpoints. *Taking Back Control: African Canadian Women Teachers' Lives and Practice.* Albany: State University of New York Press.

Hill-Collins, P. (2000). Black Feminist Thought: *Knowledge Consciousness and the Politics of Empowerment,* (2nd Ed.) New York, NY: Routledge. p.284

Hoffman, D. M. (1999). Culture and Comparative Education: Toward Decentering and Recentering the Discourse. *Comparative Education Review* 43, 4.

Hochschild, A. (1989). *The Second Shift: Working Parents and the Revolution at Home.* p. 258, 464-488. New York: Viking Press.

Hodkinson, P. and Hodkinson, H. (2004). The Significance of Individuals' Dispositions in Workplace Learning: A Case Study of Two Teachers. *Journal of Education and Work 17, 2,* 67-182.

Holland, J. (2006) *Career Web and Interests.* http://www.student.services. wiu.edu/careers/decision/interestgame.asp

hooks, B. (1988). *Talking Back.* Toronto: Between the Lines.

hooks, bell. (2000). *Feminism is for Everybody: Passionate Politics.* Cambridge, MA: South End Press.

hooks, B. (2004). *Teaching to Transgress: education as a practice of freedom.* New York: Routledge.

Hoopes and Pusch. (1984). *Global Guide to International Education.*

Hout, M. (1984). Occupational Mobility of Black Men. *American Sociological Review, 49,* 308-322.

Human Resource Management Organization., (2006). HRMO Survival Guide - Career ladders, September, 2006, from http://www.rdc. noaagov/~hrmo/ HRMOSurvivalGuide/ career-ladders.htm

Human Resource Village., (2000-2007). *HR Toolkit.* October, 2006, from http://www.hrvillage.com/human-resources/definition.html

International Council of Nurses. (2006). *Career Development in Nursing*, October, 2006, from http://www.icn.ch/pscardev.htm

Jackson, S. (2003). *Lifelong Earning: working class women and lifelong learning. Gender and Education 15*, 4, 365-376.

Jacobs, J. (1961). *The Death and Life of Great American Cities*. New York: Random House.

James, C. E. (1996). *Perspectives on Racism and the Human Services Sector: A Case For Change*. Toronto: University of Toronto Press.

James, S.M. (1994). Mothering: A Possible Black Feminist Link to Social Transformation? In S. M. James and P.A. Busia (Eds.). *Theorizing Black Feminisms: The Visionary Pragmatism of Black Women*. New York, NY: Routledge.

Jencks, C. (1992). *Rethinking Social Policy: Race, Poverty and the Underclass*. Cambridge, MA: Harvard University Press.

Jencks, Christopher & Peterson, Paul (Eds.). (1991). *The Urban Underclass*. Washington, DC: Brookings Institute.

Jenkins, R. (1992.) *Pierre Bourdieu*. London: Routledge.

Jones, Effie H, Montenegro, Xenia P. (1983). Factors Predicting Women's Upward Career Moblity in School Administration. *Journal of Educational Equity and Leadership, 3, 3*, 231-41.

Kadushin, A. (1976). Men in a Woman's Profession. *Social Work, 21,* 41.

Kanter, R. (1977). *Men and Women of the Corporation*. New York: Basic Books.

Kaparou, Maria, Bush, Tony. (2007). Invisible Barriers: The Career Progress of Women Secondary School Principals in Greece. *Compare: A Journal of Comparative Education, 37, 2,* 221-237.

Kaplan, C. (1994). The Politics of Location as Transnational Feminist Practice, in I. Grewal and C. Kaplan (Eds.). *Scattered Hegemonies: Postmodernity and Transnational Feminist Practices*. Minneapolis: University of Minnesota Press.

Kehoe, W. and Mansfield, Earl. *The Limitations of Multicultural Education and Anti-Racist Education*. British Columbia.

Kimmel, M. S. (2000). *The Gendered Society*. Cambridge, Oxford: Oxford University Press. p. 41, 177, 188, 189.

Kindleberger, C.P. (1973). *The World in Depression, 1929-1939*. Chicago: University of Chicago Press.

King, J. E. (1999). In Search of Method for Liberating Education and Research: The Half [That] Has Not Been Told. In C. A. Grant (Ed.).

Multicultural Research: A Reflective Engagement with Race, Gender, Class and Sexual Orientation. Philadelphia: Farmer Press.

Klein, J. (1980). *Jewish Identity and Self-Esteem.* New York, NY: Institute on Pluralism & Group Identity, American Jewish Committee.

Kurian, G.T. (1998). *World Education Encyclopedia.* Detroit: Gale Group.

Kymlicka, W. (2002). *Contemporary Political Science 2nd Ed.* Cambridge Oxford: Oxford University Press.

Lacey, C. (1977) *The Socialisation of Teachers.* London: Methuen.

Ladd, E. C. (1999). *The Ladd Report.* New York: Free Press.

Lampkin, Lorna. (1985) "Visible Minorities in Canada." *Equality in Employment: Research Studies.* Ottawa: Minister of Supply and Services, p.677.

Langston, D. (1998). *Class and inequality: Tired of playing monopoly?* Dubuque, IA: Kendall-Hunt.

Lather, P. (1986). Issues of Validity in Openly Ideological Research: Between a rock and a Soft Place. *Interchange* 17, 4, p.74.

Lather, P. (1998). Critical pedagogy and its complexities: a praxis of stuck places. *Educational Theory, 48,* 487-497.

Lave, J. & Wenger, E. (1991). Situated Learning. Cambridge, Oxford: Cambridge University Press.

Lawn, M. (1981). *Modern Times?Work, professionalism and citizenship in teaching.* Falmer Press.

Learning for Life Resource Center (2008). *Explore Careers and Plan for the Future.* January, 2008 from http://www.learning4liferesources.com/ free_career_planning_sites.html

Leithwood, K. A. & Reihl, C. (2003). *What we know about successful leadership?* Brief Prepared for the Task Force on Developing Research in Educational Leadership, Division A of the American Educational Research Association.

Lenskyi, Helen. (2004). *A Lot to Learn.* Toronto, Women's Press.

Lewis, G., P. Holland, and K. Kelly. (1992). *Working-class students speak out.* Radical Teacher.

Li, Peter S. (1999). *Race and Ethnic Relations in Canada,* (2nd Ed.). Cambridge, Oxford: Oxford University Press.

Lindle, J. (1994). *Surviving School Micropolitics.* Lancaster: Technomic.

Lindle, J. (1999). What can the study of micropolitics contribute to the practice of leadership in reforming schools? *School Leadership and Management 19,* 2, 172.

Livingstone, D. W. (1987). Class Ideologies and Education Futures. London : Falmer Press. p. 62

Livingstone, D.W. (2004). *The Education-Jobs Gap: Underemployment or Economic Democracy.* Aurora, ON: Garamond Press.

Livingstone, D.W. and Peter Sawchuk. (2004). *Hidden Knowledge-Organized Labour in Information Age.* Aurora, ON: Garamond Press.

Lopez, G. R. (2003). The (Racially Neutral) Politics of Education: A Critical Race Theory Perspective. *Educational Administration Quarterly 39, 1,* 68-94.

Lorbiecki, A. & G. Jack, (1999). *Critical turns in the evolution of diversity management,* paper presented at the British Academy of Management annual conference. Manchester.

Lott, B. (1987). *Women's Lives: Themes and Variations in Gender Learning.* Brooks/Coles. Monterey, CA.

Lucey, H. & D. Reay, (2000). Social class and psyche, *Soundings* 15, Summer, 139-154.

Luhmann, N. (2006). "System as Difference." *Organization Journal 13, 1.*

MacBeath, J. (2005). "Leadership as distributed: A matter of practice". *School Leadership and Management, 25, 4,* 349-366.

MacLeod, J. (1995). *Ain't No Makin' It: Attainment in a Low-Income Neighborhood.* Boulder: Westview Press. p. 15.

Maguire, M. (1998). *Not footprints behind but footsteps forward: working class women who teach.* London: King's College Press.

Maguire, M. (2001). The cultural formation of teachers' class consciousness: teachers in the inner city, *Journal of Education Policy, 16, 4,* 315-331.

Mann, M. (1970). The Social Cohesion of Liberal Democracy. *American Sociological Review, 35,* 423-439.

Mann, C. (1998). The impact of working class mothers on the educational success of their adolescent daughters at a time of social change. *British Journal of Sociology of Education*, 19, 2, 211-226.

Marginson, S. (1993). *Education and Public Policy in Australia.* Cambridge: Cambridge University Press.

Marginson, S. and M. Mollis. (2001). The Door Opens and the Tiger Leaps: Theories and Reflexivities of Comparative Education for a Global Millennium. *Comparative Education Review 45, 4,* 581-615.

Merriam, S. B. & E. Simpson. (2000). *A Guide to Research for Educators and Trainers of Adults.* (2nd Ed.) Florida: Kreiger Publishing Co. p. 5

Merton, R. (1968). *Social Theory and Social Structure.* New York: The Free Press.

Miles, A. (1998). North American Feminist/Global Feminisms: Contradictory or Complementary? In O. Nnaemeka (Ed.), *Sisterhood, Feminisms and Power: From Africa to the Diaspora*. Trenton NJ: Africa World Press.

Miller, S. (1983). *Men and Friendship*. Boston: Houghton Mifflin

Mincer, J., (1962) "On-the-job training: Costs, Returns and Some Implications," *Journal of Political Economy*, pt. 2, p. 50-79.

Miner, A.S., Estler, S.E. (1985). Accrual Mobility: Job Mobility in Higher Education through Responsibility Accrual. *The Journal of Higher Education, 56, 2,* 121.

Ministry of Information and Natural Orientation. (2007). *About Ghana-Education-Ministries-Minister*. February, 2006, from http://www.ghana.gov.gh/governing /ministeries/social/education.php

Minors, A. (1996). *From Uni-versity to Poly-versity Organizations in Transition to Anti-Racism*. Toronto: University of Toronto Press.

Moulton, J., K. Mundy, M. Welmond & J. Williams. (2002). Education Reforms in Sub-Saharan Africa: Paradigm Lost? Contributions to the Study of Education. *Comparative Education Review, 82.*

Moureau, M.P., Osgood, J., Halsall, A. (2007). *Making Sense of the Glass Ceiling in Schools: An Exploration of Women Teachers' Discourses. Gender and Education, 19, 2* 237-253.

Mullaly, B. (2002). Challenging Oppression: A Critical Social Work Approach. Cambridge, Oxford: Oxford University Press.

OECD. (1997). Education at a Glance.

OECD. (2007) Internationalization of Higher Education in the OECD Countries: Challenges and Opportunities... van der Wende *Journal of Studies in International Education.*2007; p. 8-11

Offer, A. (2006). The Challenge of Affluence. Self-control and well-being in the United States and Britain since 1950. Oxford: Oxford University Press.

Office for National Statistics. (2001). *Social Capital: A review of the literature*, London:

Office for National Statistics.

Okano, K. (1993). *School to Work Transition in Japan*. Clevedon: Multi-Lingual Matters.

Omi, M. & Winant, H. (1992). Racial Formations. In Race, Class and Gender in the United States: An Integrated Study. (Ed.). Paula S. Rothenburg, New York, NY: St. Martin's Press.

Ontario Ministry of Education., (2006). *Education Update.*, March, 2006, from http://www.edu.gov.on.ca/eng/general

Organisation for Economic Co-operation and Development (1997a). *Thematic Review of the First Years of Tertiary Education.* Paris: Directorate for Education, Employment, Labour and Social Affairs.

Organisation for Economic Co-operation and Development (1997b). *Internationalisation of Higher Education.* Paris: Centre for Educational Research and Innovation.

Ozga, J. & Lawn, M. (1981). *Teachers, professionalism and class.* London: Falmer.

Pahre R. (2005). *Leading Questions: How Hegemony Affects the International Political Economy.* Detroit, MI: University of Michigan Press.

Parkin, F. (1971). *Class inequality and political disorder.* St. Albans: Paladin Books.

Perron, A. (2010). *TCDSB Director's Voice-Beginning of the Year Address.* www.tcdsb.org

Pheterson, G. (1990). Alliances Between Women: Overcoming Internalized Oppression and Internalized Domination, in Lisa Albrecht and Rose M. Brewer (Eds.). *Of Power: Women's Multicultural Alliances* (pp. 34-48). Gabriola Island, B.C.: New Society Publishers.

Pinderhughes, E. (1989). *Understanding Race, Ethnicity, and Power: The Key to Efficacy in Clinical Practice.* New York, NY: The Free Press. p. 109

Politt, K. (1997). *Killer Moms, Working Nannies",* The Nation.

Portes, A. (1998). Social Capital: Its Origins and Applications in Modern Sociology. *Annual Review of Sociology, 24,* 1–24.

Prentice, S. (2000). *The Conceptual Politics of the Chilly Climate Controversies.* Fredricton, Manitoba: University of Manitoba Press. p. 198

Priola, V. (2007). Being Female Doing Gender. Narratives of Women in Education Management. *Gender and Education, 19, 1,* 21-40.

Prospero, Moises. (2007). Dos Hermanas Chicanas: Overcoming Barrier to Professional Advancement. *Aztlan: A Journal of Chicano Studies, 23, 2,* 47-63.

Putnam, R. D. (1993). *Making Democracy Work. Civic traditions in modern Italy,*

Princeton NJ: Princeton University Press.

Putnam, R. D. (1995). Bowling Alone: America's Declining Social Capital. *Journal of Democracy 6, 1,* 65-78.

Putnam, R. D. (2000). Bowling Alone: The collapse and revival of American community. New York: Simon and Schuster. p. 19

Putnam, R. D. (Ed.). (2002). *Democracies in Flux: The Evolution of Social Capital in Contemporary Society.* New York: Oxford University Press.

Rex, John. (1991). *Ethnic Identity and Ethnic Mobilisation in Britain.* Centre for Research in Ethnic Relations, University of Warwick.

Rainbird, H. (2000) Skilling the Unskilled: Access to Work-Based Learning and the Lifelong Learning Agenda. *13, 2,* 183–197.

Ramsay, P. (1983). Fresh Perspectives on the School Transformation-Reproduction Debate: A Response to Anyon from the Antipodes. *Curriculum Inquiry. 13, 3,* 295-320.

Rao, A., Rieky Stuart, and David Kelleher. (1999). *Gender at Work: Organizational Change for Equality.* West Hartford, CT: Kumarian Press. p. 3

Rappaport, J. (1985). The Power of Empowerment Language. *Social Policy* 16, 2, 15-21.

Razack, S. (1998). *Looking White People in the Eye.* Toronto: University of Toronto Press.

Reason and Rowan. (1981). *Human Inquiry: A Sourcebook of New Paradigm Research.* New York, NY: John Wiley & Sons.

Rees, R. (1990). *Women and Men in Education: A National Survey of Gender Distribution I School Systems.* Toronto: Canadian Education Association. p. 102

Reskin, B. (1996). *Women and Work: A Handbook.* New York, NY: Garland.

Reynolds, M. and K. Trehan, (2001). Classroom as real world: Propositions for a pedagogy of difference. *Gender & Education* 13, 4, 357-72.

Ringrose, J. (2007). Successful Girls? Complicating Post-Feminist, Neoliberal Discourses of Educational Achievement and Gender Equality. *Gender and Education, 19, 4,* 471-489.

Robertson, C. (1984). Formal or Non-Formal Education: Entrepreneurial Women in Ghana. *Comparative Education Review 18, 4,* 639-658.

Rose, M. (2001). Working Life of a Waitress. *Mind, Culture and Activity,* 6.

Ross, P. (1987). Women, oppression, privilege and competition. In V. Miner & H. Longino, (Eds.), *Competition: A Feminist Taboo?* New York: Feminist Press.

Ryan, R. & Deci, E.L. (2000). Self-Determination Theory and the Facilitation of Intrinsic Motivation, Social Development and Well-Being. *American Psychologist* 55.

Ryan, J. (2003). Dealing with Dilemmas of Difference: Two Cases. In J. Ryan, *Leading Diverse Schools.* Dordrecht: Kluwer.

Ryan, J. (2005). *The inclusive leadership framework*. Paper presented at the annual meeting of the Canadian Association for Studies in Educational Administration. London, Ontario.

Sawchuk, P. (2006). Frameworks for Synthesis in the Field of Adult Learning Theory *Contexts of Adult Learning: Canadian Perspectives*.

Siu, R. G. H. (1979) *The Craft of Power*. New York, NY: John Wiley & Sons.

Schugurensky, D and K. Mundel. (2005). Voluntary Work and Learning, *International Handbook of Educational Policy*. p. 12

Schultz C. & Sherman, R. (1976). Social Class, Development and Differences in Reinforcer Effectiveness. *Review of Education Research*, *46*, 25-59.

Schultz, T. W. (2006) "Investment in Human Capital." *American Economic Review*, 51(1): p.1.

Sennett, R. (1998). The Corrosion of Character. The personal consequences of work in the new capitalism. New York: Norton.

Sergiovanni, T.J., Kelleher, P., McCarthy, M. & Wirt, F.M. (2004). *Educational Governance and Administration*, (5th Ed.). Boston: Pearson Publishing.

Sfard, A. (1998). On Two Metaphors for Learning and the Dangers of Choosing Just One. *Educational Researcher 27, 2*, 4–13.

Shapiro, J.S. (1958). *Liberalism: its meaning and history*. Toronto:D.Van. Norstrom Company.

Shapiro, J.P. & Stefkovich (1998). Dealing With Dilemmas in a Morally Polarized Era: The Conflicting Ethical Codes of Educational Leaders. *Journal for a Just and Caring Education. 4, 2*, 117-141.

Shapiro, J.P. & Stefkovich, J.A. (2005). *Ethical Leadership and Decision-Making in Education* (2nd Ed.). New Jersey: Lawrence Erlbaum Associates.

Sharp & Greene (1975) The Impact of the Student Teaching Experience on the Development of Teacher Perspectives, Journal of Teacher Education, op. cit., vii, p. 234

Sirianni, C. and Friedland, L. (undated). 'Social capital', *Civic Practices Network*, http://www.cpn.org/sections/tools/models/social_capital.html

Skocpol, T. (2003). Diminished Democracy. From membership to management In American civic life, Norman: University of Oklahoma Press.

Sleeter, C. (1999) Writing from the Heart. In C. A. Grant (Ed.). *Multicultural Research: A Reflective Engagement with Race, Gender, Class and Sexual Orientation*. Philadelphia: Farmer Press.

Sleeter, C.E. & Grant, C.A. (2003). *Making Choices for Multicultural Education: Five Approaches to Race, Class and Gender* 4th Ed. New York, NY: Wiley.

Slogan, D. (1993). *A Reader in Feminist Ethics*. Toronto: Canadian Scholars' Press.

Small, S. (1994) Racialised barriers: the black experience in the United. Winant *Prog Hum Geogr*. pp. 19, 441-442

Smith, D. (1977). *Feminism and Marxism: a place to begin, a way to go*. Vancouver, BC: New Star Books.

Smith, D. (1987). *The everyday world as problematic: A feminist sociology*. Toronto, University of Toronto Press.

Smith, D. (1990). *The conceptual practices of power: A feminist sociology of knowledge*. Toronto, University of Toronto Press.

Smith, T. L. (1999). *Decolonizing Methodologies: Research and Indigenous Peoples*. New York, NY: St. Martin's Press.

Smith, M. K. (2007). Social capital. *The encyclopedia of informal education*. www.infed.org/biblio/social_capital.htm p. 1

Solomon, R. P. (2002). School Leaders and Antiracism: Overcoming Pedagogical and Political Obstacles. *Journal of School Leadership*. Toronto: York Press.

Sonnenfeld, J. A. (1989). *Managing career systems: channeling the flow of executive careers*. Irwin.

Spence, C. (2009). *Leading with Passion and Purpose, Pembroke Publishing, p. 37.*

Springer, K. (2002) Third Wave Feminism? *Signs: Journal of Women in Culture and Society, 27, 4,* 1059-1082.

Strauss, A. and J. Corbin. (1990). *Basics of Quantitative Research: Grounded theory procedures and techniques*. Newbury Park, CA: Sage.

Starratt, R.J. (1991). Building an Ethical School: A Theory for Practice in Educational Leadership. *Education Administration Quarterly 27, 2,* 185-202

Starratt, R. J. (2004). *Ethical Leadership*. San-Francisco: Jossey-Bass.

SWAOC Video - Social Work Anti-Oppression (2006). "On the Road to Becoming Anti-Oppressive: Peers Teaching Peers. Toronto: Ryerson University School of Social Work.

Stewart, Lee. (1990). *"It's Up to You": Women at UBC in the Early Years* Vancouver: University of British Columbia Press, p. 4

Stewart, T. A. (1999) *Intellectual Capital: The New Wealth of Organizations.* New York: Doubleday.

Syed, Z., Hyles, D. & Jenkins, A. (2006). Race to the Top Case Study. p. 1-3.

TDSB P/VP Promotion Diversity Stats 2010-11. (2011). TDSB Spring and Fall Rounds.

The Concise Encyclopedia of Economics. (2008). Theodore Schultz Biography. February, 2008, from www.econlib.org/library/Enc/bios/Schultz.html

The World Bank (1999) 'What is Social Capital? *PovertyNet* http://www.worldbank.org/poverty/scapital/whatsc.htm

Tomlinson, C.A., Demirsky, S.A. (2000) *Leadership for Differentiating Schools & Classrooms.* Alexandria, Va: Association for Supervision and Curriculum Development. p. 46

Tosey, P. & S. McNair, (2000). Work related learning, in P. Jarvis (Ed.). *The Age of Learning: education and the knowledge society.* London: Kogan Page.

Toronto Board of Education (TBE). (1975) *The Bias of Culture: An Issue Paper onMulticulturalism.*Toronto: Toronto Board of Education.
(1979) *Final Report of Sub-Committee on Race Relations.* Toronto: Board of Education.
(1984) *Race Relations Program: Phase II.* Toronto: Toronto Board of Education.
(1989) "Handling Racial Incidents." Toronto: TBE.
(1993) "Elementary Student Demographics." Toronto: TBE Research Services.

Toronto Catholic District School Board. (2006). *History of Catholic Education.* January, 2006, from www.tcdsb.org/

Toronto District School Board. (2006). *History of Public Education and Hiring Policy.* January, 2006, from www.tdsb.on.ca

Troyna, B. (1994) *Reforms, Research and Being Reflexive about Being Reflexive.* In D. Halpin and B. Troyna (Eds.). *Researching Education Policy: Ethical and Methodological Issues.* London: Falmer Press.

UNESCO Institute for Statistics., (2006). *UNESCO country profile on Ghana and Canada.* January, 2006, from http://www.uis.unesco.org/profiles/EN/ countryPage

Vince, R. (1996). Experiential management education as the practice of change, in L. Morley & V. Walsh (Eds.). *Breaking Boundaries: women in higher education.* London: Taylor & Francis.

Vinsky, J. (2010). *Themes in Bridging Transformation.* Liberation Practice International Curriculum, p.1.

Wacquant, L. & Wilson, William Julius. "The Cost of Racial and Class Exclusion in the Inner City." *Annals of the Academy of the American and Political Sciences,* 501.

Walzer, M. (1997). *On Tolerance,* New Haven: Yale University Press.

Wane, N. Deliovsky, K. and Lawson, E. (2002). *Back to the Drawing Board: African-Canadian Feminisms.* Toronto: Sumach Press.

Wanner, R. (2005). Twentieth-Century Trends in Occupational Attainment in Canada. *The Canadian Journal of Sociology, 30, 4.*

Wells, T. (2005). Educational Policy Networks and Their Role in Policy Discourse, Action and Implementation. *Comparative Education Review, 49, 1.* p. 110

West, Cornel. (1993). *Race Matters.* New York, NY: Vintage House: A Division of Random House.

West, M. (1999). Micropolitics, leadership, and all that ... The need to increase the micropolitical awareness and skills of school leaders. *School Leadership and Management 19,* 2, p. 191.

Wheatley, M. (1992). *Leadership and the New Science.* San Francisco: Berrett-Koehler.

Willis, P. (1997). *Learning to labour: how working class kids get working class jobs* Aldershot: Saxon House.

Williams, C. (1995). The Glass Escalator: Hidden Advantages for Men in the "Female Professions. *Journal on Social Problems.* p. 296.

Wikipedia the free Encyclopedia., (2006). *Education in Ghana.* January, 2006, from http://en.wikipedia.org/wiki/Ghana

Woolcock, M. (2001). The place of social capital in understanding social and economic outcomes. *Isuma: Canadian Journal of Policy Research 2, 1,* p. 13.

Wotherspoon, T. (2004) Chapter 6: Schooling and Work. *The Sociology of Education in Canada.*

Wright, E. O. (1985). *Classes.* London: Verso.

Wuthnow, R. (1998). *Loose Connections: Joining Together in America Fragmented Communities.* Harvard: Harvard University Press.

Yeskel, F. (1990). *Understanding class and classism.* Unpublished paper. Amherst, MA.

Zald, M. & M. Berger. (1994). Social movements in organizations: Coup d'etat, bureaucratic insurgency and New Brunswick: Transaction Publishers. p. 202

Zimmer, L. (1998). Tokenisms and Women in the Workplace: The Limits of Gender-Neutral Theory. *Journal on Social Problems 35, 1,* 64.

Zimmerman, E. (2004). The Puzzle of System Transformation: Towards an Explanatory Sketch. *Comparative Sociology Journal 3, 4.* p. 286

INDEX